THE ULTIMATE SERIAL KILLER TRIVIA BOOK

Scary Stories, Frightening Facts, and Deadly Details That Are Guaranteed to Send a Chill Down Your Spine

Damian Dark

© **Copyright** 2020 - All rights reserved.

The content contained within this book may not be reproduced, duplicated or transmitted without direct written permission from the author or the publisher.

Under no circumstances will any blame or legal responsibility be held against the publisher, or author, for any damages, reparation, or monetary loss due to the information contained within this book, either directly or indirectly.

Legal Notice:

This book is copyright protected. It is only for personal use. You cannot amend, distribute, sell, use, quote or paraphrase any part, or the content within this book, without the consent of the author or publisher.

Disclaimer Notice:

Please note the information contained within this document is for educational and entertainment purposes only. All effort has been executed to present accurate, up to date, reliable, complete information. No warranties of any kind are declared or implied. Readers acknowledge that the author is not engaged in the rendering of legal, financial, medical or professional advice. The content within this book has been derived from various sources. Please consult a licensed professional before attempting any techniques outlined in this book.

By reading this document, the reader agrees that under no circumstances is the author responsible for any losses, direct or indirect, that are incurred as a result of the use of the information contained within this document, including, but not limited to, errors, omissions, or inaccuracies.

TABLE OF CONTENTS

Introduction 1

Chapter 1: Hunting Serial Killers 5

Chapter 2: Roots of Evil 20

Chapter 3: General Serial Killer Trivia 43

Chapter 4: Infamous Serial Killers 48

Chapter 5: Female Serial Killers 73

Chapter 6: Serial Killers Across the Globe 96

Chapter 7: Lesser-Known Serial Killers 113

Chapter 8: Unsolved Serial Killer Cases 133

Chapter 9: Killer Couples 165

Chapter 10: When Children Kill 193

Conclusion 211

References 219

Image References 220

INTRODUCTION

The woman picks up her pace as her gut starts to tell her something is wrong. She's jogged in these woods many times before, and she is intimately familiar with its noises. She knows what the squirrels sound like when they scamper through the brush, and she also knows that there is other wildlife that share this forest—mountain lions and bears—although she's never encountered one.

As she casts a glance behind her, she is sure that a dark shadow moves between the trees that line her path. Options race through her mind. Should she leave the path and attempt to navigate the dense tree line? Should she start sprinting in the hopes that whatever is lurking nearby will not be able to catch up? What she doesn't know, as visions of carnivorous predators flash through her mind is that there is a different kind of predator hunting in these woods. He is not following the instinct of a mountain lion to kill for survival. Instead, he is driven by the most warped of instincts—he kills for pleasure.

Her body will be found by a dog walker three months later, and her family's hope for her safe return will be dashed. Law enforcement will spread out through the woods like ants seeking evidence to identify her killer, but what they find will be much worse. There are more. Spread throughout the undergrowth, police will uncover four more deceased women. All had been dragged off the trail, violated, bound, and strangled.

***

Although I cannot say for sure that it was just this case that had piqued my interest in serial killers, it certainly played a major role. The murders occurred near my hometown, in forests that I had played in as a child. I was getting ready to graduate and head off to college when this series was revealed, and as I followed media reports, I couldn't help but wonder what type of person does this.

That perpetrator was never identified, he just faded away, and the vicious murders remain unsolved to this day. At the time, I had thought that he must have just decided to stop killing, and every time I walked past someone on the street, I wondered if it was them. Years later, I now know that serial killers do not simply stop killing. The seemingly unfathomable desire that drives them never goes away. From that day on, I have devoured every piece of information I can find about the minds of these men and women who hunt others.

Many of my friends and family members do not understand my interest in serial killers. They think it's dark and maybe a little twisted to be so interested in what the world sees as inexplicable evil. Throughout my research, though, I have found that many others are as interested in serial killers as I am. Our need to know more about these people is not morbid or driven by sensationalism. We simply want to find an answer to the overriding question here—why?

Why do some people hunt others? Why do they continue to do so even when it is very clear that they are going to be caught? What makes a seemingly normal child grow up and become a monster?

It is for this reason that I decided to put together *The Ultimate Serial Killer Trivia Book*. Rather than being the story of one or two infamous serial killers, it is a collection of facts and tidbits from all the research I have done throughout the years. If, like me, you are serial killer obsessed and not ashamed to say so, you are about to have questions answered that you didn't know existed.

As you delve into the information presented in this book, it is important to me that one thing is always kept in mind—the victims. Although this book predominantly focuses on the killers themselves, I do not believe in glorifying these predators. Behind every serial killer name or moniker there are countless human beings who lost their lives in horrific and terrifying ways. Their families have forever been changed by the actions of these men and women, and it is vital that, as purveyors of this information, we always keep that in mind. The pain and suffering that each of the cases we discuss in this book represents can never be forgotten.

Our interest in serial killers must therefore be aimed at increasing the knowledge pool around these frightening criminals so that the loss of their victims can be channeled back into understanding and preventing these crimes.

CHAPTER 1
HUNTING SERIAL KILLERS

Long before the term "serial killer" was ever coined, those to whom we entrust our safety have been hunting men and women who kill multiple victims. As we have come to better understand the motives, modus operandi, and inner workings of serial killers, our knowledge base has grown, and the way we investigate serial crimes has changed. Hunting down a serial killer is very different from other homicide investigations in many ways. Although the main principles of the investigation such as victimology, focusing on those closest to the victim, and evidence collection remain the same, when dealing with a purely psychological motive, things get a little more difficult. In this chapter, we will explore the methods and practices used in tracking down, arresting, and convicting serial killers.

Q: What is the difference between serial killers, mass murderers, and spree killers?

Throughout the last few decades, various schools of thought in criminal psychology have developed different definitions for these three types of murderers.

Famed profiler Robert K. Ressler, who coined the term "serial killer" when he worked for the Federal Bureau of Investigations (FBI), developed probably the most comprehensive definitions with his research partner, Tom Schatman, in 1993.

The pair defined a **serial killer** as a person who kills more than three victims during three or more events, and often at three or more locations. There is usually a cooling-off period in between the murders, and elements of fantasy and premeditated planning are also present. It is easy to see how serial killers like Ted Bundy and Ed Gein, for instance, would fit into this definition.

A **mass murderer**, in Ressler and Schatman's definition, is a person who kills four or more victims in a single event, at a single location. The tragic school shootings we have seen, particularly in the United States, during the last few decades fit this description perfectly. If we look at the Columbine school massacre, which is probably the most infamous of all such crimes, perpetrators Eric Harris and Dylan Klebold shot and killed 12 students and 1 teacher in a single, planned event on the 20th of April 1999 at their school in Columbine, Colorado.

Spree killers are often confused with mass murderers, but the definition of their crimes is quite distinct. Ressler and Schatman define spree killers as one or more people who commit two or more murders during an event at two or more locations. There is no cooling-off period during the spree. Andrew Cunanan is an infamous example of a spree killer. Cunanan killed five people, including Italian fashion designer Gianni Versace, over a three-month period in 1997. Most spree murders happen over shorter periods than Cunanan's crimes as the perpetrator will be triggered by a specific event and ride that wave until he burns himself out or is arrested. One of the major reasons that Cunanan's crimes and those of most spree killers are not classified as serial killings is because of the nature of the motive. While not all serial killers' crimes are spurred by fantasy, Cunanan's murders were almost nonsensical in nature and predominantly rage driven.

Image 1: Crime scene tape

Q: How are serial killers classified by those that hunt them?

As part of our pool of knowledge around serial killers, and in order to help identify them, investigators use four criteria to classify a serial offender:

- **Victimology:** the characteristics of the victims, how they are chosen, and any relationship they have with the offender
- **Background** of the offender's behavior
- The **pattern and method** of the crimes
- **Locations** of the murders: are they concentrated or dispersed?

By using these criteria, serial killers are placed in one or more of the following types:

- **Mission-oriented:** these serial killers will murder according to a mission they have created in their minds. A killer who sets out to wipe out all sex workers, for instance, will fit into this type.
- **Visionary:** these killers often have some form of delusion present, and they believe that they are acting on the orders of some other entity such as God or a demon. Often though, visionary serial killers do not suffer from any mental health issues, and they have, instead, created this idea in their heads to absolve themselves from their crimes.

- **Power/control:** this is often the type of serial killer who commits sexual crimes in addition to murder, and their victims will often be women. They kill to satisfy a deep-seated need for control over life and death. Strangulation is a common method of killing with these types as they have ultimate control over when the victim dies.

- **Hedonistic:** this type is broken down into three further categories: sensation, lust, and comfort (Pistorius, 2005).

Q: What is the difference between an organized serial killer and a disorganized one?

Ressler and Schatman developed some criteria for deciding whether a serial offender could be considered organized or disorganized.

With organized serial killers, you will generally see an increase in planning with each murder, while disorganized serial killers will often become more erratic and less careful as their desire to kill increases. The organized killer is far more likely to have a fantasy that they use as a type of blueprint for their murders, and they select their victims according to a specific criterion. The organized killer uses the victim's humanity against them and will often interact with them and use confidence tricks to gain their trust. Organized serial killers adapt well, take weapons with them to the scene, and make sure that they remove as much evidence as possible. Organized murderers often rank far higher on the psychopathy checklist than disorganized serial killers (Pistorius, 2005, 2006).

Q: At what stage in an investigation does law enforcement acknowledge that they are investigating a serial killer?

In most cases, the first indication that a serial killer is at work will be a forensic or behavioral link between two crimes. So, if DNA is found at a murder scene and it is found to match DNA at another murder scene, police will know they have a serial offender on their hand. This comparison, though, would not necessarily be done unless there appears to be a similar modus operandi (method of operation).

A single homicide will be investigated as exactly that until evidence is found to prove that the way in which a victim was killed is similar to that of another, the location is the same, or the victimology matches up. Ordinarily, only then will DNA comparisons be made.

It is far easier for police to identify a series where the killer is taking victims frequently, and those victims live a low-risk lifestyle. Unfortunately, many serial killers know very well that high-risk victims such as sex workers or homeless people will likely not be identified as part of a series really quickly.

When a series of murders spreads across a relatively large geographical area, and different law enforcement agencies are involved, this makes it even more difficult to confirm a series because these agencies don't always communicate effectively.

Q: What is a task force, and how is it used in serial murder investigations?

A task force is a group of law enforcement professionals and sometimes outsourced experts that is brought together to investigate a particular crime or series of crimes. It will often include members from many different agencies and disciplines, and the skills of the members will complement each other.

The task force will be headed by one particular senior member who will usually be the most experienced in investigating the type of crime in question. Task forces will form in different stages of investigations and will grow or shrink in numbers depending on the amount of time that passes as well as the number of victims. A task force will usually have a specific headquarters to work out of and information about the case as well as photographs of the victims will be displayed around the room.

Image 2: Forensics

Q: What are some of the databases that a task force will use in a serial killer investigation?

Throughout the years, various databases have been built to assist in investigations. These databases bring information on a wide range of cases and perpetrators to one single resource, allowing investigators to do legwork that would take months in the click of a button. Types and qualities of databases differ around the world. In the United States, which has the highest number of serial killers globally, the following databases are available to investigators:

- The Combined DNA Index System (**CODIS**): this is a database that contains the digital representations of DNA samples from across the United States. It includes DNA from convicted offenders, crime scenes, and unidentified persons.

- The Automated Fingerprint Identification System (**AFIS**): this database contains fingerprints from unsolved cases and convicted offenders, as well as from federal employees and first responders whose fingerprints may be left at a crime scene through their work there.

- The National Integrated Ballistics Identification Network (**NIBIN**): this database contains images of bullets and projectiles recovered from other crime scenes. In the case of a serial killer who uses a gun, their crimes could be linked by running an image of a bullet recovered from a victim through this database to find a match to previous crimes.

- The National Missing and Unidentified Persons System (**NamUs**): this database helps investigators if they have victims that are unidentified. As victimology is such an important part of solving a case or a series of cases, if victims are unidentified, it makes the police's job all the more difficult. NamUs contains profiles of identifying information of missing, unclaimed, and unidentified people across the United States.

Q: What is profiling and how is it used to catch serial killers?

The concept of criminal profiling was first developed by a New York psychiatrist called James A. Brussel in 1941. Brussel used a technique of analyzing communications and behaviors of a bomber who had been terrorizing New York for 16 years to draw up a report of the likely characteristics the unidentified offender would have.

When the offender in question was eventually arrested in 1957, he matched Brussel's profile exactly. It would take another 20 years for criminal profiling to start being formalized as a tool in law enforcement, though, with the pioneers of this shift being the agents at the Behavioral Sciences Unit of the FBI. The widely acknowledged definition of a criminal profile is an investigative technique through which a crime is analyzed in order to identify the major personality traits and behavioral characteristics of an offender.

The intention of a criminal profile is not to tell police who the perpetrator is, but rather to paint a picture of the type of person that would commit such crimes, and possibly provide an insight into motivation. This helps police to identify the most likely type of suspect they are looking for. If specific interests or fields of work are identified as being likely, for instance, the police will have a way to narrow their search down. Some of the serial offenders that were captured as a direct result of the criminal profiling tool include Ted Bundy, Joseph Paul Franklin, and Wayne Williams.

Q: How do police interrogate suspected serial killers?

Although the procedure and art of interrogation does not differ entirely from a single homicide to that of a serial crime, it cannot be denied that serial killers are very different from most other homicide perpetrators. Interrogating a serial killer straddles a fine line between striking while the iron is hot, so to speak, and making sufficient preparation so that the conversation goes the way police want it to. Often, police will review criminal profiles before an interrogation in order to ascertain the best way to approach a suspect.

Staging the interview room is another common practice. Investigators may place photographs of the victims, crime scenes, and murder weapons in plain view of the suspect. Often when suspects are confronted by their crimes unexpectedly, they will break down and confess. With serial killers, many enjoy discussing their crimes, and the photographs will be a trigger for them to brag about their crimes. Police may turn down the temperature in the room so that it is extremely cold, thereby making the suspect uncomfortable. This could also help the interrogators to gain confidence with the suspect by offering them a blanket or asking if they would like the temperature increased. Any small connection like this helps to build rapport between the police and the suspect.

Building rapport is a huge part of a successful interrogation, and this goes for single homicide perpetrators as well as serial killers. An element of trust needs to be built as the killer is essentially allowing these people into the darkest parts of his mind. In the beginning, interrogators will ask really easy questions, often not even related to the crimes. These questions are used to lull the suspect into a sense of security, so that later on, when the tough questions are asked, they will be more likely to answer honestly.

Q: Do serial killers want to get caught?

One of the greatest myths that surrounds serial killers is that, whether consciously or subconsciously, they want to get caught by police. This myth probably comes from the crimes of disorganized serial killers where their actions are so seemingly rash and brazen that one must assume they are trying to get themselves arrested. This is certainly not the case. Although many serial offenders have been known to express relief at being caught after some time in prison, that is only because they have been relieved of the opportunity to act out their compulsions, and not because they didn't want to kill in the first place.

It is perhaps simplistic to say that serial killers enjoy killing, as "normal" people like you and I equate "enjoyment" with wholesome activities. For a serial offender, though, their sense of enjoyment has become warped, and instead of being linked to activities like spending time with family or eating delicious foods, their pleasure sensors are triggered by the act of killing. There is, therefore, no reason that they would want to give up that sense of enjoyment.

Q: Which serial killer evaded capture for the longest time?

In the United States, at least, it seems to be a toss-up between Samuel Little and Joseph DeAngelo. Of course, there are many serial killers who have remained at large for far longer than these two. Samuel Little was convicted of three murders in 2014. He then began to confess to a lot more, and it has been determined that he started killing in 1970.

Joseph DeAngelo's crimes started in 1975, and he was arrested in 2018.

The simple truth is that there are many serial killers still on the loose, and that number grows daily. Serial killers generally do not stop killing unless they are somehow restricted either by incarceration, disability, or age. Joseph DeAngelo, for instance, admitted that the only reason he had stopped was because he realized that he was getting too old to overpower his victims. Whether this is true or not remains to be seen. When a serial killer appears to stop, it is far more likely that the killer has either changed their modus operandi so drastically that their crimes are no longer linked, or they have simply moved geographical areas.

CHAPTER 2
ROOTS OF EVIL

One of the reasons that we are drawn to stories about serial killers is because we want to understand why they do what they do. We want to try and comprehend how a relatively normal little boy or girl grows up to be a vicious killer. Throughout the last few decades, many different schools of thought have tried to tackle the question of whether a killer is made or born. While the nature versus nurture debate rages on, we do seem to be arriving at a relatively accurate conclusion. The truth is that every killer is different, and it is impossible to develop one overriding theory that fits each one. In this chapter, we will delve into some of the theories that have been formed over the years and try to understand what makes serial killers tick.

Q: Are all serial killers psychopaths?

Mainstream media has turned the word "psychopath," or its shortened version, "psycho," into a term we use regularly, and almost always incorrectly. When we think about a psychopath, we envision a raving lunatic who is not in control of their own faculties and who lashes out at the nearest person to satisfy their violent fantasies. This could not be further from the truth.

In order to understand why we cannot classify all serial killers as psychopaths, we must first understand the true definition of the word. Psychopathy is actually not a clinical diagnosis, and no psychiatrist will ever diagnose a person as being a psychopath. Rather, it is just one of the elements of antisocial personality disorder which in itself is also not considered a mental illness. A person with antisocial personality disorder may be described as having psychopathic traits or tendencies. These tendencies are measured by using a tool called the Psychopath Checklist.

Some of the traits exhibited by such people include:

- Behavior that is considered socially irresponsible

- Violating or disregarding the rights of others, often in the respect of the person not actually acknowledging that others do have rights. They may also assume that their rights are superior to those of others

- An inability to distinguish right from wrong. This, however, is not because they do not know that certain things are right from a societal perspective, and other things are wrong, but rather that they do not see how these rules apply to them. The fact that a person with psychopathic traits who has committed a crime seeks to hide that crime proves that they know that what they have done is not acceptable in the eyes of society.

- Difficulty showing empathy or remorse. This is often due to the person's inability to acknowledge others as being important. In the psychopath's mind, your pain does not count as much as their desire to inflict it.
- A tendency to lie.
- A tendency to hurt and manipulate others.
- Recurring problems with the law. Very often, the antisocial behavior that people with psychopathic traits display will lead to them committing a crime. These crimes are not always violent, though.
- A general disregard for responsibility and safety.

People with antisocial personality disorder often have difficulty forming deep emotional bonds and will be impulsive and abusive.

It is important to understand that psychopaths live among us. You are very likely surrounded by a good number of people right now that would rank quite high on the psychopathy checklist. In fact, there is evidence that suggests that most psychopaths are not violent criminals. Rather, they are people who have learned to use their psychopathic traits to their advantage in business, politics, and even religious leadership roles.

Now that we understand what a psychopath truly is, we can start to understand why it would be incorrect to assume that all serial killers rank anywhere of significance on the psychopathy checklist.

Image 3: Frightening child

Q: What is the nature versus nurture debate?

The nature versus nature debate among academics and now, indeed, general society is the idea that a person must either be born with the capacity to kill gratuitously, or that desire must be instilled in them throughout their nurturing years. Put simply, are serial killers born or created?

While the debate rages on, it is becoming far clearer that it is definitely a combination between the two factors that makes all the difference. So, the answer is neither and both. Pretty scientific right?

In truth, very little related to human consciousness or the development of what we call the "mind" is very scientific at all. We know how the brain develops from a scientific perspective, and we know what all the parts do, but we really don't know what makes an individual the sum of those parts. Great strides have certainly been made in understanding various mental illnesses such as depression, anxiety, schizophrenia, and bipolar disorder. We can now treat these illnesses with a rather good success rate using medication and psychotherapy, but that is because all of these mental illnesses are caused by a physical disturbance, whether structural or chemical, that we can pinpoint and work toward rehabilitating. The emotional disturbances on the other side of the spectrum—personality disorders—often do not have a diagnosable cause, and neither do they have a treatment. The fact that far more convicted serial killers have personality disorders rather than mental disorders underlines for us that we cannot really say where their problems began.

Indeed, there are serial killers who report having had the most horrendously abusive childhoods, and it's almost understandable that they would have lived some form of deviant life. I say "almost" because many of those serial killers have siblings who grew up in the same environment as them and have never so much as gotten a speeding ticket. So, what is it within that person that combined childhood trauma with some other indefinable element to create a person that is capable of such vicious deeds?

An interesting thing to consider about serial killers that grew up in abusive homes is that both mental illness and personality disorders are considered to have genetic factors involved in their development. Abusive parents would likely indicate some form of emotional disturbance there as well, so perhaps the roots go much further back than we think. Again, though, there are a huge number of people who experience traumatic childhoods and do not become serial killers.

It is also important to understand that each serial killer is an individual, and the origins of their deadly intentions will always differ. In general, it is probably fair enough to answer the nature versus nurture question with:

Nature + Nurture + X = Serial Killer

Q: What is Robert Ressler's motivational theory around serial killers?

Famed profiler Robert Ressler and his colleagues at the Behavioral Sciences Unit at the FBI conducted interviews with 36 incarcerated serial killers. The research they gleaned from these interviews was combined into a model which Ressler hoped could be applied to individual cases to gain a greater understanding about the origins of serial killers.

The model consisted of five different categories of research:

- formative years
- efficacy of social environment
- actions toward and treatment of others
- patterned responses
- feedback

Ressler explored the impact the serial killers' social environments had during their formative years and found that in many cases, as children, the killers formed limited bonds with their parents or caregivers. This often occurred because their parents would either ignore or normalize unacceptable behavior. One example is how Jeffrey Dahmer's father did not think it was strange that his son was dissecting animals in his bedroom.

The study also found that 25 of the 36 serial killers reported have alcoholic or drug-addicted caregivers. Psychiatric problems were also common within the family, and, interestingly, many of the killers' mothers had been institutionalized for periods of time.

The father's role in the serial killer's life was also investigated, and it was discovered that the physical presence of a father figure did not have as much impact as emotional presence. An abusive father that lived in the home did far more damage than an absent father did.

As far as abuse during formative years, Ressler found that the biggest difference between the average person who may have been abused during their childhood and a serial killer who experienced the same was the fantasies that the child developed to escape from the abuse. Most children who are living in abusive situations will fantasize about escaping the situation. Children who grow up to be serial killers will have violent fantasies about ways in which they can regain control in the situation they are in. When these children are having these fantasies, they feel powerful for the first time, and they will become attached to these thoughts for this reason. These are often the same fantasies that will play out when they are adults in their murders.

The patterned responses that Ressler observed in many of the subjects he interviewed were closely linked to these fantasies. The serial killers would find themselves in cognitive loops where they would continually relive their fantasy until such point that the inner stress became too great, and they had to act it out.

Due to their personality disorders, serial killers will often see other people simply as an extension of their inner world, and this can even start when they are children. When a serial killer commits their first murder, they begin to give themselves internal feedback on how well they did.

While many agree with much of what Ressler has included in his model, some disagree that it is possible to isolate motivation down to a conscious thought level. Most serial killers are not terribly self-aware and cannot even describe their urge to kill adequately.

Q: Do some serial killers get arrested multiple times?

While almost globally it is acknowledged that serial killers cannot be rehabilitated and once they are imprisoned, they will likely never be paroled, there are many cases in which systemic failures have resulted in serial killers being arrested mid-series and then released only to continue killing.

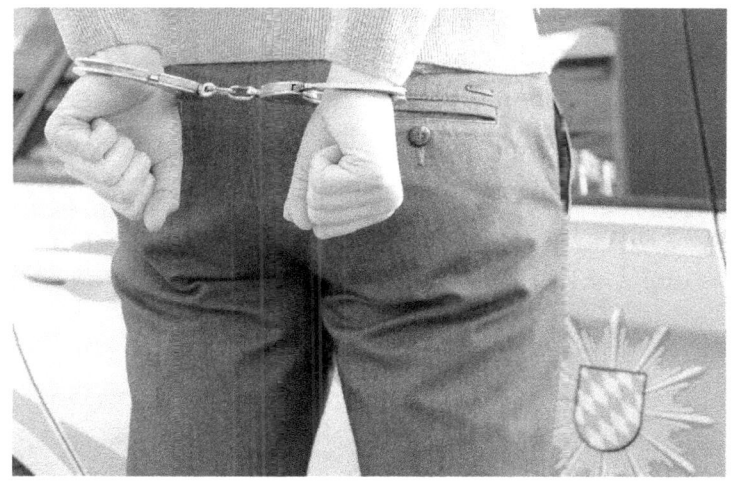

Image 4: Arrested

One example of this is Jeffrey Dahmer. Dahmer was charged with possession of child pornography in 1989. A psychologist recommended that he be remanded to an institution until he was rehabilitated as it was believed that he had the potential to offend again. His defense attorney said the following, "We do not have a multiple offender here. I believe he was caught before the point where it would have gotten worse" (Pistorius, 2005).

What no one in that courtroom knew was that Jeffrey Dahmer had already killed five people by that point. He was sentenced to one year in jail for that crime but was on day-release so he could go to work. He was also given five years' probation, and his probation officer would later admit that he thought something was wrong, but he did not investigate further because, on the surface, Dahmer was complying with his probation conditions. On the 26th of May, 1991, a member of the public found a young man called Konerak Sinthasomphone naked and drugged on the street. The police were called, and the two officers, believing that they were witnessing a lovers' quarrel, ignored Konerak's pleas for help, and took him back to Dahmer's apartment! The young man was killed just a few hours later. In the three years that Dahmer was out on probation, he killed another 11 young men.

Q: Do serial killers play up to the media?

It is a well-known attribute of some serial killers (and other murderers) to insert themselves into the investigation of their murders, as well as to enjoy the limelight they are receiving.

For most of these people, this is the first time in their lives that they have been seen as "special," albeit in a rather heinous manner, and many of them lap up the attention that the media gives their crimes. The monikers that serial killers are given to identify them before they are arrested are often coined by the media to increase the terror element among their readers. Some serial killers have gone so far as to indicate what they want their own moniker to be, which proves that they have a deep need for this kind of recognition. David Berkowitz only started calling himself "Son of Sam" after a newspaper reporter used this moniker in an article.

Robert Ressler discovered in his interviews with serial killers that many would avidly follow newspaper coverage and even cut out and keep articles related to their crimes as trophies.

The power of the media became quite evident in Berkowitz's case when he acknowledged that he had only gotten the idea to start committing murders in each county after a reporter had published information about each of the cases and speculated about whether the killer would start to kill in the remaining areas. This coverage had further knock-on effects when it would later be discovered that Monty Rissell had gone on to murder five women because, he claimed, he was inspired by the notoriety that "Son of Sam" was gaining in the media.

Q: What is the Macdonald Triad?

Forensic psychiatrist J. M. Macdonald developed a triad of behaviors in 1963 which he believed, when present in childhood, were indicators of that child becoming a murderer as an adult.

The three behaviors are:

- animal cruelty
- fire-setting
- bed-wetting

This triad has since been applied in many investigations and analyses of murderers and serial killers. As our pool of knowledge around these matters has grown, though, it has become increasingly clear that the triad is not a particularly useful diagnosis tool. The pool of research candidates that Macdonald used was nowhere near large enough, and many of them had actually never committed a violent offence; they had simply verbalized violent fantasies.

In 2009, PhD student Kori Ryan conducted the most extensive review of all literature in this field to date (Ramsland, 2012). The results of this PhD study showed that there is very little evidence to support the predictive value of the Macdonald triad. The behaviors mentioned show that a child is stressed or has poor coping mechanisms but certainly does not indicate the child will become a serial killer. In most of the serial killers interviewed by Robert Ressler, only one of the behaviors, or sometimes none, were present in childhood.

Q: Do all serial killers have a fantasy that drives them to kill?

While this has long been the overriding belief and it certainly has been shown that most serial killers do have some form of fantasy that drives them, not all do. For many serial killers, there are specific elements of the crime that excite them, and it is not always the act of killing. Very often the run-up to the crime, including stalking and victim selection, is the most exciting part of the murder. For sexually driven killers, it is often the control they exert over their victims that is the most enjoyable act.

Even serial killers that go into a crime with a very specific fantasy, which they have developed in great detail, will change that fantasy slightly as they continue to commit murders. This is why forensic profilers do not look for scenes that are identical, but rather for a repetition of elements. Victims do not need to be tied up in exactly the same way, for instance, for it to be the same killer. Bondage is one particular element of a fantasy that does tend to change as a killer may have a fantasy going in about what they want, but quite by chance, they may figure out that some other form of control excites them more. When a profiler or investigator looks at a string of murders in chronological sequence, they will be able to identify the progression that the perpetrator is making in their modus operandi as their fantasy changes.

Q: Do serial rapists always become serial killers?

While not all serial rapists progress to murdering their victims, when they do it is usually for one of two reasons. Often the control that they are getting from the rape act itself is no longer sufficient to feed their desire, and killing becomes the ultimate act of control. The other reason is that they have been convicted for one or more of their rapes, and while in prison, they have made the decision that when they get out they will permanently silence their victims so that they will be less likely to get caught.

Joseph DeAngelo, now known as the Golden State Killer, started his crime spree with burglaries. He quickly escalated to raping his victims and the further escalated to murder. For DeAngelo, the reason for his progression was clearly an increased need for control.

Even in perpetrators who remain rapists and never progress to murder, their modus operandi changes slightly, and they will often start to use more violence in their crimes as they progress.

An example of a serial rapist who progressed to murder after being imprisoned is notorious South African serial killer, Moses Sithole. Sithole committed three rapes in the late 1980s and was sentenced to 10 years for one of these crimes. On his release after serving seven years of his sentence, Sithole decided that he would simply eliminate the possibility that any of his victims could ever testify against him, and he began to kill the women that he raped. Sithole would go on to be convicted of 38 murders and 40 rapes, but it is believed that his victim count was far higher than that (Pistorius, 2005).

Q: Are all serial killers male?

The answer to this question is definitely not. In fact, female serial killers are so prevalent that we have an entire chapter in this book dedicated to them. Female perpetrators make up about 17% of all serial killers in the United States (Bonn, 2014).

The myth surrounding the gender of serial killers is perpetuated by the media, as even women who kill are almost always presented in books and movies as submissive victims of the manipulation of a man. Aggression and violence are simply not equated with the female image in society, and this adds to our aversion to considering women as possible predators.

Q: Are all serial killers reclusive loners who stand out as being "weird"?

Again, the media plays a role in perpetuating this myth as serial killers are presented as psychotic misfits who hide in their mothers' basements and only come out at night to kill. This image could not be further from the truth. Most serial killers blend very well into society and are gainfully employed, and many even have families.

This chameleon-like ability to blend in is one of the things that makes many serial killers so successful. They have the ability to disarm their victims simply because they look and act like the average Joe next door. Much of this ability stems from an element of antisocial personality disorder, ironically. While one would think that such a disorder would make it more difficult for the serial killer to act like everyone else, as people with antisocial personality disorder get older, they become very good at observing those around them and understanding how they should be acting in order to blend in. Such people are also very good at manipulation, and that is another way that they get people to let their guards down.

While for many of these people this facade of normality is all on the surface, and as soon as you start to dig a little deeper their true nature is revealed, there are just as many who have sewn this deceptive thread throughout their lives. This is often to such an extent that their partners, children, and extended family have absolutely no idea how depraved they are. An excellent example of this is Dennis Rader, the BTK killer. Rader was married to his wife for 34 years and had two adult children by the time he was arrested for his crimes in 2005. Although his wife would mention small instances of strange behavior that he had displayed throughout the years, in general, she had no idea that he was capable of such heinous acts. His children describe him as a loving father who they looked up to. The only people who really knew what Dennis Rader was were his victims.

Q: Do all serial killers travel a lot and kill their victims across state lines?

While much has been said about the existence of hundreds of interstate truck drivers who are also serial killers and commit their crimes along their routes, this type of serial killer is actually extremely rare. More often than not, serial killers will operate in a well-defined geographical area in which they feel comfortable. This is usually down to convenience, but it is also because the killer knows the area well enough to have easy access to resources they need to accomplish the crime. They will be able to more easily stalk and surveil future victims, they will be able to carry their weapons of choice with them, and they know which areas are best for disposing of bodies.

Another benefit for the killer of operating within an area that they are familiar with is that they also become aware of how law enforcement in that area operates. They will know which areas are monitored by police and at what times, and they will also know the type of victim that is likely to not be missed for an extended period of time. Although law enforcement is pained to admit it, there is a certain amount of victim profiling that comes into play when police decide which missing people are considered endangered. This profiling is based on the missing person's risk profile, and it is not uncommon for little effort to be put into a missing person's case where the person is a sex worker, drug addict, homeless person, or teenager who has a history of running away. Even the community they live within is taken into consideration.

Often the geographical area in which a killer operates is determined by their own anchor point such as where they live or work. One example of a deviation from this general rule is Israel Keyes. Keyes is believed to have been responsible for at least 11 murders within the United States possibly dating back as far as 1996. Keyes traveled for work, and he went to great lengths to ensure that he could kill without detection no matter where he was. This planning included burying what he described as "kill kits" when he visited specific areas so that when he returned there, he would have what he needed to commit his crimes. In this way, Keyes made many geographical areas comfort zones for himself.

CHAPTER 3
GENERAL SERIAL KILLER TRIVIA

Now that we have delved into the roots and investigation of serial murders, in this chapter we will zoom in on some specific individuals and their crimes.

Q: What is what of the most famous quotes from a serial killer?

One of the most famous serial killer quotes of all time comes from Ted Bundy when he was attempting to bring across the ease with which serial killers infiltrate society. He was certainly the "man next door" and managed to live a rather high-profile life and ingratiate himself into society. The quote reads as follows:

"We serial killers are your sons, we are your husbands, we are everywhere. And there will be more of your children dead tomorrow."—Ted Bundy.

Q: Who was the first person to be considered a serial killer?

H. H. Holmes, who was active in the 1880s, is considered to be the first serial killer in the United States. He admitted to killing 27 people in his Chicago hotel. Global history goes back much further than that, though, with anecdotal evidence pointing to instances of serial murder as far back as the 5th century AD. Dhu Shanatir was a king who lived in what is now considered Yemen, around this time. He is alleged to have sexually assaulted and murdered more than 100 young boys before being stabbed by his last victim.

Q: What professions do the most prolific serial killers come from?

Ironically, health care workers, including doctors and nurses, top the list where the most prolific serial killer professions are concerned. Although the thought that someone that has taken an oath to heal would purposefully harm is difficult to comprehend, if we consider the relationship between doctor and patient, it is perhaps not difficult to understand how it may happen. We trust both doctors and nurses, almost implicitly. We would likely not think to question anything they do as we see them as far more qualified than ourselves. If a doctor tells you that you need an injection, you stick your arm out. Generally, you don't question what is in the syringe, and even if you did, you would have no way of knowing if the doctor was indeed telling the truth.

Image 5: Healthcare worker

It is this implicit trust that predatory health care workers have used in the past to carry out their murderous intentions. Later in the book, we will discuss female serial killers, and many of those were nurses. Probably the most famous serial killer doctor is Britain's Dr. Harold Shipman. Although Shipman was only convicted of killing 15 patients, an inquest would later find significant evidence to prove that he could be responsible for up to 250 murders. If this number is accurate, he would be the most prolific serial killer in modern history. Shipman was a trusted local doctor and known to the elderly community as being a doctor with a wonderful bedside manner. He also did house calls which gave him access to his patients' personal lives. His modus operandi was to ingratiate himself to his victim and then administer a huge dose of morphine to cause their death. In many cases, Shipman had either convinced his elderly patients to make him a beneficiary in their will, or he had forged wills to secure their money for himself.

Having detailed knowledge of the human body as well as having access to many types of legal and deadly drugs also make healthcare workers particularly dangerous when they turn rogue.

Q: What was the San Quentin Bridge Club?

Image 6: Playing cards

In 1990, *Vanity Fair* magazine published an article which revealed that in the late 1980s four infamous serial killers had all been housed in California's San Quentin State Prison. William Bonin, Randy Kraft, Lawrence Bittaker, and Douglas Clark were also all avid bridge players, and the four serial killers had formed their own bridge club. The club broke up when William Bonin was executed (Philbin & Philbin, 2009).

CHAPTER 4
INFAMOUS SERIAL KILLERS

In this chapter, we will look at some of the most infamous serial killers in history. Serial killers become well-known for many reasons. For some, it is because of the number of victims they have killed. For others, it is simply their peculiar strangeness or how horrendous their acts were. Sadly, the infamy that these serial killers gain is the most attention many of these people have had in their entire lives, albeit negative attention. To them, though, it doesn't seem to matter. Most of the murderers we will discuss in this chapter very much enjoy the media attention they receive as well as the continued attention their crimes receive after they are apprehended. This is, of course, the nature of narcissistic personality disorders, to which many serial killers are subject. For these people, fear is the same thing as respect, and the more revolting their crimes, the more respect they believe they deserve. You will very likely have heard many of the names that will be mentioned here, but I am certain that you will learn some new facts about these frightening predators and their crimes.

Q: Who was one of the first serial killers to taunt his victim's family by mail?

Albert Fish was a serial killer who operated between 1924 and 1932. He was convicted of one murder which would eventually send him to the electric chair, but he alluded to being involved in over 100 murders across the United States.

Image 7: Mailboxes

Today, it is not uncommon for us to see single-crime killers and serial killers taunting surviving victims or deceased victims' families by email or telephone calls, but in the 1930s when Albert Fish kidnapped 10-year-old Grace Budd, it was a sickeningly new trend. In 1928, Fish took little Grace from her parents' home under false pretenses. They never saw the child again. In 1934, an anonymous letter was sent to the Budd family, which later turned out to have been written by Fish. In it, he detailed how he had killed Grace, and sickeningly, also admitted to having cannibalized her remains. It would be this letter that eventually led to Fish's arrest after an eagle-eyed detective managed to identify an emblem on the paper which led him to Albert Fish. Grace Budd's skull was eventually recovered outside the residence where Fish had killed her (Philbin & Philbin, 2009).

Serial killers often get great satisfaction out of sending communication to victims' families, the police, and the press. It is believed that the creation of these communications provides them with a sense of power and enables them to relive their crimes as they write or speak about them. This compulsion has also led to the arrest of many serial killers including Dennis Rader, who was eventually arrested in 2005 after a long period of silence when he wrote a letter to police and sent it to them on a floppy disk. Police used the metadata in the document to trace the author. After having been active from 1974 to 1991, Radar had reemerged in 2004 and attempted to take responsibility for deaths which were proved not to be linked to him. Had his own narcissistic desires not overtaken him, he would likely never have been caught.

Joseph DeAngelo also enjoyed taunting his victims, and many of his surviving victims recounted receiving calls from the man many years after their attack. He would whisper ominously into the phone, "I'm going to kill you." DeAngelo went as far as tracking his victims after they had moved and calling them on new numbers just to terrify them even more as they realized that their attacker was still hunting them.

Many serial killers enjoy communicating with the media as they are aware that this is their best chance at gaining notoriety. Probably the most famous example of this is the still unsolved case of the Zodiac killer. The Zodiac is believed to have killed anywhere between 5 and 37 victims in the 1960s and 1970s. He sent several letters to journalists as well as ciphers or cryptograms. We will find out more about the Zodiac killer in our chapter on unsolved serial murders.

Q: Which offender believes that a motorcycle accident made him a serial killer?

While it is not uncommon to discover head injuries in the histories of serial killers or other violent offenders, this is never believed to have been the only contributing factor to serial murder. One infamous serial killer, though, points to a head injury incurred in a motorcycle accident as a turning point in his life, which he believes led to his crimes (Philbin & Philbin, 2009).

Bobby Joe Long was executed by lethal injection in 2019. He was convicted of killing 10 women between March 1984 and November 1984 and raping one surviving victim. He is believed to have raped many more women before his killing spree began. Although most serial killers are unable to determine the point at which their life changed paths, Long was always convinced that his troubles had started in 1974 when he had a motorcycle accident. He claims that after receiving a head injury his sex drive increased tremendously to the point where sex was all he thought about. His wife at the time would confirm that their marital relations had increased in frequency from two to three times per week to two to three times per day, every single day. In addition to this, Long claimed that he was also masturbating up to six times a day. He says that soon relations with his wife were insufficient to sate his need, and he began to seek out other women. Between 1980 and 1983, Long embarked on an extensive serial rape spree. He claims that another side effect of the head trauma he experienced was that he would experience bouts of uncontrollable anger. It would be this anger, he claimed, that eventually resulted in him killing his first victim after raping her. He would go on to kill nine more women before being captured in November 1984.

While certain traumatic brain injuries (TBI) have been known to result in increased levels of impulsive and aggressive behavior, this is not true for all TBIs, and for those who do experience this it can be managed and often recedes with therapy and the natural healing process. There are, in fact, many serial killers who have reported experiencing TBIs before commencing their murderous criminal careers, but a report in the Journal of Neuropsychiatry and Clinical Neurosciences concludes that there may be a very different reason for this (Mosti & Coccaro, 2018).

In many patients who committed violent crimes after experiencing a TBI, research into the patients' histories showed that they had exhibited impulsive and aggressive behavior before the TBI as well. Aggressive and impulsive behavior often starts very early in life, and it is the very nature of this type of behavior that may result in the person finding themselves in a situation where they may experience a TBI. Most TBIs occur as a result of an assault or in a car or motorcycle accident at high speeds. While we cannot say that any person deliberately puts themselves into a position where they will be assaulted, it is fair to say that if a person is aggressive, a bar fight, for instance, may more likely result in a more severe incident than if the person did not display aggression. Impulsive and risk-taking behavior such as speeding or not wearing a seat belt or a helmet on a motorcycle can also result in an increased likelihood of a TBI. It is therefore far more likely that serial killers, including Bobby Joe Long, who experienced TBIs were already exhibiting levels of aggression before the incident, and the injury simply accelerated a downward spiral that was already in motion.

Q: Which infamous serial killer's victims looked extremely similar?

Victim selection is more important to some serial killers than others. For some serial killers this is the most exciting part of the crime, and they are very specific about the type of victim they select. For other serial killers, the type of victim is less important than their availability. In most cases, at the very least, gender and race will remain consistent among victims, but there are certain instances where even this is not relevant to the killer.

One of the most infamous serial killers whose victim selection seemed to be very precise is Ted Bundy. Although we don't really know for sure exactly how many women Ted Bundy killed, he confessed to having killed 30. All the confirmed victims look extremely similar. Most were young females in their late teens or early twenties. They were almost all brunettes and had shoulder-length or longer hair that they wore parted in the middle. All had similar, attractive facial features and were diminutive in build. Looking at photos of all of his victims, the similarity seems undeniable, but Bundy insisted that it was not intentional. He said that he chose victims who were available to him at the time, and he didn't care what they looked like. Perhaps for Bundy, who presented himself as a rather intelligent man, admitting to focusing his kills on something as superficial as appearance, felt beneath him. Many people have pointed to the fact that a middle hair parting was a popular hairstyle at the time, but the other similarities between his victims cannot be ignored.

During an investigation, victim selection can often be a sign of escalation. If a killer suddenly starts selecting victims that are very different to earlier victims, it can be a sign that their compulsion is starting to take over, and they can no longer wait to find the "perfect" victim. In these cases, victims will generally still be the same gender and often race, but their age range and appearance may differ significantly. This change in victim type will also be accompanied by a reduction in the cooling off periods between the crimes.

Sometimes serial killers only realize in the midst of their murders that they actually prefer a certain type of victim to one they may have started out with, and investigators will then see a shift in victim selection.

Image 8: Toolbox

An example of a very specific targeting mechanism by a serial killer is the case of Lawrence Bittaker and Roy Norris, who were nicknamed the Toolbox Serial Killers. We'll talk more about Bittaker and Norris in our chapter about Killer Couples, but their intention in victim selection is certainly worth mentioning here. After their arrest, the pair claimed that their plan was to kidnap, torture, rape, and kill one girl for every year of a teenager's life. They would ultimately end up killing five girls over a four-month period in 1979, aged 13, 15, two girls aged 16, and one aged 18. The truth behind this plan, though, was simply that Bittaker, who was the more dominant of the two, was sexually attracted to teenagers, and Norris simply went along with the idea. Whether it somehow seemed more "noble" in their minds to have this grand plan, both would admit that once they had a girl in their grasp, it didn't matter how old she was.

Possibly one of the strangest examples of specific victim selection can be found in a serial murder case from 1942. An American soldier in Australia, Eddie Leonski, killed three women before being apprehended. He claimed that he selected his victims by the sound of their voice. If he came across a woman whose voice he liked, he would kill her as he hoped to be able to "own" her voice after her death.

Q: What were Ted Bundy's final moments like?

Arguably one of the most notorious serial killers in history, Ted Bundy's execution was awaited with great anticipation by the families of his 30 named victims, as well as the general public. While it may seem odd to anticipate the death of a man, Bundy was unlike most other men. His brutality and the callousness he showed his victims had not only made him one of the world's most hated men but also an enigma that was greatly feared, and still is to this day.

The day before his execution, Bundy was interviewed by psychologist James Dobson. Dobson would later relay that Bundy had spent most of the interview complaining about how his addiction to pornography had ruined his life. About halfway through their conversation, the lights in the prison momentarily dimmed. Bundy told Dobson not to worry, he was familiar with this occurrence in the run-up to executions. The prison officials were testing the electric chair for Bundy's own execution the following day (Philbin & Philbin, 2009).

Bundy phoned his mother twice that night. He refused to choose his own final meal, and so he was given the standard last meal of eggs, hash browns, steak, and toast. He is alleged to have barely eaten any of it and was likely hungry when he was strapped to the electric chair.

On the day of Bundy's execution—January 24, 1989—a large group gathered outside the prison gates chanting "Burn, Bundy,

Burn!" There were also millions of viewers watching the televised proceedings from home. During his reign of terror, Bundy famously broke into the Chi Omega sorority house on the Florida State University campus and murdered two sorority sisters, Margaret Bowman and Lisa Levy. He also attacked another three women who barely escaped with their lives. The Chi Phi fraternity house held a celebratory barbeque on the day that Bundy was executed. They served "Bundy burgers" and "electrified hot dogs." The fraternity house was adorned with a banner which read "Watch Ted fry/See Ted die" (Margaritoff, 2019).

Forty-two people came to witness Ted Bundy's electrocution. including experts who had worked with him in prison, detectives who had worked his cases, and family members of his victims. His final words were, "I'd like to give my love to my family and friends."

He was pronounced dead at 7:16. am.

Q: How are infamous serial killers remains dealt with after they die?

For most serial killers, whether they die of natural causes in prison or they are executed, there is no ceremony or public display of affection for them after they leave this Earth. In many cases, the brains of serial killers are removed after their death for scientific research.

Ted Bundy's brain was also removed after his electrocution in the hopes that scientists might be able to uncover some abnormality that could have caused his murderous rampage. None was found. Bundy received a far kinder send off than he perhaps deserved. His final wish was for his ashes to be scattered in Washington's Cascade mountain range, and this is indeed what was done. It is unknown how his victims' families may have felt about this considering he used this very same area to dump four of his victims.

When Charles Manson died in 2017 at the ripe old age of 83, a group of friends and supporters set up a crowdfunding donations page to raise funds to give the alleged cult leader and convicted murderer a proper burial. The effort was shut down within hours. In California, where Manson was imprisoned, next of kin are given 10 days to present themselves and claim the body of an offender. If this does not happen, the deceased is cremated.

British serial killer, Ian Brady, whose crimes we will discuss in more detail in our Killer Couples chapter, died in prison at the age of 79 from natural causes. A High Court judge ruled that Brady's remains should be disposed of without any "music or ceremony." As a result of this judgment, Brady's body was taken under police escort to a crematorium where he was cremated. His ashes were then placed in a weighted biodegradable urn and disposed of at sea by authorities in the dead of the night. The reason for this judgment having been passed down was that there was concern that his remaining next of kin may scatter Brady's ashes at Saddleworth Moor where he had buried many of his victims. As at least one of his Brady's victims still remains undiscovered to this day, the possibility that a murderer may be laid to rest in the same place as his victim was more than anyone could bear.

When Brady's partner in crime, Myra Hindley, died in 2002, authorities attempted to arrange burial for her in an undisclosed location, but 20 funeral directors who were approached to facilitate the burial all refused. The final resting place of Hindley is unknown.

Jeffrey Dahmer's parents argued for some time about what to do with his remains after he was beaten to death in prison by a fellow inmate. His brain was removed and preserved in formaldehyde. His mother wanted scientists to be able to determine whether there was a biological cause for her son's heinous acts, but his father insisted that Dahmer had wanted his entire body cremated. A judge would eventually side with the father, and his entire body was cremated, and the ashes were split between his parents.

John Wayne Gacy, who murdered at least 33 people, also had his brain removed after death, and the rest of his body was cremated. A psychiatrist, Helen Morris, who worked with Gacy's defense team was given the brain to analyze, and it is alleged that she keeps it stored in her basement for further research.

Q: Which infamous serial killer was killed by his own victim?

On the 8th of August 1973, police in Texas received a call from one Wayne Henley. The young man told police that they should come to the address he provided as he had just killed a man.

The story that unraveled from that point was almost too strange for belief. Henley, it turned out, had been assisting a man called Dean Corll for three years to lure young boys to his home. Although he initially believed that Corll was raping and releasing the victims that he brought to him, he soon realized that the older man was in fact murdering many of them. It would eventually emerge that Dean Corll had raped, tortured, and murdered at least 28 young boys and men in his home between 1970 and 1973. On the morning of his own demise, Corll had been angry with Henley because he had brought a female friend into the house. Corll had handcuffed Henley, the girl, and another young male present and threatened to kill them all. Realizing that he needed to turn the tables on Corll in order to survive, Henley had convinced the man that, as penance, he would help him kill the other two if he just uncuffed him. As soon as the cuffs were off, Henley grabbed a nearby gun and emptied six bullets into Dean Corll.

Corll is certainly not the only serial killer to have been taken down by an intended victim though. In 2015, Neal Falls was shot and killed by a sex worker he had tried to kill. Heather Saul had invited Falls into her home for a sexual encounter and he had immediately held her at gunpoint. A struggle had ensued which resulted in Falls receiving a single gunshot wound to the head. Only after his death were police able to link Falls to several murders, and it became clear that the brave woman had, in fact, stopped a serial killer in his tracks.

A serial killer known as the Missoula Mauler is believed to have killed at least five people between 1974 and 1985. The man, Wayne Nance, was never arrested despite compelling evidence linking him to the very first murder committed in the series. Justice would eventually be delivered by another intended victim when Nance broke into the home of Kris and Doug Wells in 1986. He attacked the couple in their bedroom, and despite stabbing Doug in the chest, the man was able to retrieve a gun from his nightstand and fire a bullet into Nance's head, killing him instantly.

Q: Have any serial killers kept their victims captive for long periods before murdering them?

While most serial killers prefer to kill their victims almost immediately, others get great pleasure from prolonging the suffering and have been known to hold victims captive for days, weeks, and even months, before eventually killing them.

Gary Heidnik was arrested in 1987 after police found that he had been holding six women captive in his basement for months. He had raped, tortured, starved, and beaten all of the women and killed two of them. The four survivors spoke of the horrors they had experienced while being imprisoned in Heidnik's home including having to witness the murder of two of their cocaptives. This modus operandi was not new for Heidnik, and he had committed a similar crime in the past but unfortunately been released from jail, only to continue with the same behavior. Heidnik was eventually convicted of the rapes and murders and sentenced to die by lethal injection. The sentence was carried out on the 6th of July, 1999 (Philbin & Philbin, 2009).

Israel Keyes's last victim, Samantha Koenig, was held for a day in his shed before he killed her, but Keyes was able to convince Samantha's family as well as police that she was alive for almost three weeks after her death. After killing Samantha, Keyes left her body in his shed. He lived in Anchorage, Alaska, where temperatures were so low that when the killer decided to leave for a two-week holiday with his family, he returned to a frozen corpse. He later recounted to investigators that he had removed Samantha's body from the shed, applied makeup to her face, and sewed her eyelids open to make it appear as though she were still alive. He then took a photograph of her with a newspaper from that day and sent it to her family demanding a ransom. Her boyfriend would later say that he felt that something was wrong with the photograph as Keyes had fixed Samantha's hair in a way that she would never wear it.

Another serial killer who took pleasure from holding his victims captive was the Kansas City Butcher, whose real name is Robert Berdella. In 1988, Berdella was arrested and eventually found guilty of six murders and several rape charges. He admitted that he had held most of his victims captive and subjected them to torture and abuse for up to six weeks at a time.

Q: Which serial killer is known as the "Killer Clown"?

John Wayne Gacy was convicted on 33 counts of murder after his arrest in 1978. His victims were all young boys and men. During his murderous spree, Gacy often worked as a clown at children's parties and other events, and a chilling photograph exists of him dressed in full clown attire with a painted face and stony look in his eyes. Since the photograph emerged, professional clowns have come forward to state that the way in which Gacy applied makeup around his mouth is contrary to how professionals do it. In order to avoid scaring children, the line around a clown's mouth should always be rounded, but Gacy always drew the edges of his in a pointed fashion. Whether he did this intentionally or not is unknown. Gacy performed under the stage name "Pogo the Clown."

Jonathan Davis, the lead vocalist for the rock group KoRn, now owns two of Gacy's clown suits, and they are on display in his home along with other crime memorabilia that Davis collects.

Q: What are paraphilias and which infamous serial killers had them?

Paraphilic disorders occur when a person has a recurrent, intense, sexually arousing fantasy or behavior and that urge becomes distressing or disabling. Paraphilias usually involve inanimate objects, nonconsenting adults, children, or behavior that is seen as outside of social norms. Paraphilias are different from ordinary fetishes as they are intense, persistent, and often cause harm either to the person experiencing them or to others.

Paraphilic disorders often develop during childhood, and there is even evidence to suggest that certain conditions during development in the womb may contribute to the likelihood of paraphilia development. There are dozens of different paraphilias including exhibitionism, pedophilia, voyeurism, sexual sadism disorder, and pyromania.

Many serial killers have presented with specific paraphilias, especially bondage and sadism related. Albert DeSalvo, who was also known as the Boston Strangler, had a particularly brutal paraphilia for his victims. His crimes were so focused around his urge for foreign object insertion into the bodies of his victims that his only victim selection criterion was that the person be female. Between 1962 and 1964, 13 women were murdered in the Boston area who presented with the same modus operandi which would become known as Albert DeSalvo's signature. Although DeSalvo would only be convicted of one murder, he confessed to many of the 13, but his state of mind would have him initially confined to a mental institution from which he escaped after his conviction. He was then transferred to a maximum security prison and was stabbed to death by a fellow inmate in 1973.

One of the most common and disturbing paraphilias found among serial killers is erotophonophilia. This rather imposing word is even more affronting in definition. An erotophonophile is a person who has extremely violent sexual fantasies, often featuring killing their partner during sex or mutilating their genitals. This is clearly one of the most dangerous paraphilias, and such a person will find it very difficult to experience a successful sexual relationship under normal circumstances. Serial killers with this paraphilia will usually choose their victims based on their appearance or an aspect of their appearance that is arousing to them.

While shoe and foot fetishes are often made light of in society, when such a fetish becomes all-consuming in the warped mind of a serial killer, it is no longer a laughing matter. Jerry Brudos killed four confirmed victims between 1968 and 1969. In many of these cases, he retained his victims' shoes and even cut a foot off two of the bodies and kept them in his freezer. He was known to wear high heels around his home as well. After his arrest, his cell became a library of shoe catalogues, and he would allegedly write to major shoe manufacturers and request that they send him their catalogues.

Although Ted Bundy's obsession would not impact his crimes, he would reveal in interviews shortly before his death that he had an obsession with his own feet. He described them as "the most attractive feet you have ever seen" and claimed to have owned hundreds of pairs of socks.

Q: Which serial killer believed that he was driven to kill by a demon who lived inside a dog?

David Berkowitz, also known as The Son of Sam, killed 6 people and injured 10 during his reign of terror in New York between 1976 and 1977. After his arrest, he claimed that he was only following the orders of a demon. He said that the demon would settle down after he killed but then rile back up again soon after "forcing" him to kill again. His neighbor, named Sam, owned a large black dog, and Berkowitz claimed that the demon lived inside the dog. It was soon confirmed that this was just Berkowitz's attempt at an insanity defense, and he even admitted as much at one point.

Had Berkowitz not been making this up, it would have been far more likely that he was presenting with a common tendency in serial killers to name or objectify their urge to kill. Serial killers are generally not the most self-reflective of people, and often, instead of acknowledging that they simply have a deep-seated desire to kill, they will try to turn that urge into an outside force. This helps them to reduce their own culpability, at least in their minds. Many serial killers refer to their urge as a demon, another personality, or even their "boss." There is certainly no paranormal activity at work here, nor is there any form of schizophrenia or multiple personality disorders in most cases; these claims are simply the desperate attempts of a warped mind to lay blame for their crimes elsewhere.

Q: Which rock star was mistaken for an infamous serial killer?

Anthony Kiedis, the lead singer of popular rock band the Red Hot Chili Peppers, was allegedly arrested between 1977 and 1979 when police were hunting the Hillside Strangler in California and Washington. Kiedis says that he was arrested solely on the basis that he matched a sketch that had been released of the killer.

The real killers, well rather killers, were Kenneth Bianchi and his cousin Angelo Buono, Junior. We will discuss this pair's crimes in more detail in a later chapter. Thankfully for Kiedis, he had alibis for all of the times during which the murders were committed, and he was released without being charged.

CHAPTER 5
FEMALE SERIAL KILLERS

There was a time when it was believed that all serial killers were Caucasian males. Thanks to research and academic studies in the field of serial killers, though, we have come a long way in understanding that serial killers come in all shapes and sizes. Perhaps one of the most entrenched societal beliefs to break is that women are incapable of the viciousness and warped mentality that it takes to be a serial killer. The truth is that some of the worst serial killers in history are female. It is possibly the maternal nature of women that makes us believe that they couldn't possibly turn in the opposite direction and purposefully seek out and kill multiple victims. Often, as you will see in our Killer Couples chapter, when women pair up with men to kill, they will be portrayed as submissive victims of their more dominant male partners. In most cases, this could not be further from the truth.

In general, and at a global level, 95% of murderers are male (Farber, 2019, p. 213). This is often thought to be because men are more aggressive than women in general due to higher levels of testosterone. Where serial killers are concerned, 15 to 17% of all serial killers are female. In this chapter, we will discuss some of the most prolific and frightening female serial killers.

Q: Why are there fewer female serial killers than male?

Besides the biological side of it, the way that girls are raised and the norms that are placed on them by society play a major role. Females are given "permission" and encouraged to acknowledge their emotions and work through them while men are often told that it is not proper for them to display negative emotions unless those emotions enforce their manhood. When females struggle with emotions, they are far more likely to turn these emotions on themselves and self-harm or develop eating disorders or self-loathing. Men are more likely to lash out at others.

Historically, women have been seen as "paragons of virtue" and, therefore, incapable of committing heinous acts. When a woman has deviated from this norm, she has almost always been painted as "mad." As a result, most female murderers and serial killers throughout history have been made out to be victims of their own biology, rather than active participants in their own behavior (Farber, 2019).

Two studies conducted around murders committed by females have arrived at interesting conclusions regarding how the motives for murder differ between the genders. A study conducted at Pennsylvania State University looked at 64 American female serial killers. Another study conducted in Australia looked at 149 homicides in that country committed by both genders. Both studies sought to identify similarities and differences in the way men and women kill, and their motives for their crimes. Both studies reached the conclusion that, in general, "men kill for sex, and women kill for money" (Farber, 2019). This is perhaps simplistically stated, but it is a fair determination. In most cases when women kill, they do so to gain some sort of resource. Of course, as we have already learned from serial killers in general, the "hard and fast" rule does not always apply. As you will see in this chapter, there have been many female serial killers throughout history who have simply killed for the pleasure of doing so or for similar motives to their male counterparts.

Q: What type of woman is the "stereotypical" female serial killer?

Image 9: Femme fatale

In the study conducted at Pennsylvania State University, the large majority of female serial killers studied were well-educated, had caregiving roles such as nurses, teachers, stay-at-home mothers, and were predominantly Caucasian. This last criteria must be tempered by the understanding that non-White people were not offered the same educational and occupational prospects as White people in most countries across the world for a very long time, and as this starts to change, we will likely see a more diverse group of female serial killers forming.

Female serial killers almost always kill victims that they know or who are close to them. This is in contrast to male serial killers who are more likely to kill strangers. The study also found that in almost all the cases, female serial killers focused on either children or the elderly or infirm. One of the most common methods of killing seen in female serial killers is poison. In older cases, this would have been poisons that were readily available at the time like strychnine or arsenic, and as these substances have become more highly regulated and less readily available, female serial killers have moved on to substances like morphine and rodent poisons.

Q: Which is one of the earliest known cases of a female serial killer in the United States?

Jane Toppan was a nurse in Massachusetts in 1901 who eventually confessed to killing up to 30 people. Toppan used her profession to gain access to morphine and other deadly substances. Most of her victims were patients in her care, but she was also found to have killed her foster sister and a friend from her childhood. Toppan's pattern of killing is common for a poisoner. Often, they will have had thoughts about poisoning people from childhood already and will start experimenting with those closest to them. Whether such people choose to move into the healthcare profession due to their depraved interests is debatable, but it seems logical that someone who wishes to have such ultimate control over life and death would choose such a profession. Toppan allegedly told police that her ambition had always been to "have killed more people than any other man or woman who ever lived."

Toppan, who was born Honora Kelly, had an extremely difficult childhood with her mother having died when Toppan was only six years old and her father having given her and her sister up to an orphanage. Toppan would eventually go on to be an indentured servant to the Toppan family, and she took their surname as her own.

Interestingly, despite the idea that female serial killers kill predominantly for gain of some kind, there appeared to be a lust element to Toppan's murders. She admitted that she had fondled her victims while they were dying and she had gained a sexual thrill from being able to take her victims to the brink of death and bring them back, only to kill them.

This paraphilia around control may well have developed during Toppan's formative years as she was carted around between orphanages and had no sense of stability. Sometimes when children live in circumstances like this and also have other predispositions to the development of paraphilias, as they near puberty they will start to link the powerful feeling of control with sexual arousal. As a result, they may develop a paraphilia around control and power over others.

Q: Who was the Death House Landlady?

Dorothea Puente ran a boarding house in Sacramento, California, during the 1980s. The boarding house was meant to be specifically for the elderly and infirm.

On the 11th of November, 1988, police knocked on the door of the boarding house and asked Puente if she knew the whereabouts of a tenant called Alberto Montoya, who was developmentally disabled and had schizophrenia. His social worker had reported him as missing as he hadn't attended their sessions for several days. The police noticed several areas of disturbed soil in the front yard, and they began to dig. They would eventually unearth seven bodies on the property. Probably due to her "nice old lady" appearance, police initially did not think that Puente could be a suspect, so she was allowed to leave the property while the dig took place. Puente fled to Los Angeles and attempted to hide out with a friend. She would eventually be arrested, though, and charged with nine murders. Puente was 60 years old when she was arrested, and it emerged that she had primarily been killing for financial gain, as she continued to collect the disability and pension grants of her victims for many years after they had died.

It was believed that Puente had killed most of her victims by overdosing them, but this was very difficult to prove due to the advanced state of decomposition of the body and the fact that many of her victims were drug users to begin with. Puente claimed innocence and said that all of the people had died either at their own hands or of natural causes and that she had only arranged for them to be buried on her property. She would eventually only be found guilty of three of the murders, but this was enough to sentence her to life imprisonment. Puente spent 24 years in prison before dying of natural causes at the age of 84.

Q: Who is the most infamous female serial killer?

Aileen Wuornos is arguably the most infamous of all female serial killers, but this may certainly have more to do with how much her life and crimes have been covered in the media, and even in movies, than the actual crimes themselves.

Wuornos killed seven men in one year between 1989 and 1990 by shooting them at point blank range. She would attempt to claim that she had been acting in self-defense as the men had been clients (Wuornos was a sex worker), and they had attempted to rape her. The evidence, however, told a different story, and she was eventually convicted of murdering six of the men. She was executed for her crimes in 2002, and in the following year, a movie about her life and crimes was released which painted the woman as a confused and ultimately murderous victim of an abusive childhood and adult life. The abuse she experienced could not excuse her actions, though, and the murders she committed were believed to be her way of taking back control.

Q: Which female serial killer targeted her romantic partners and her own son?

Judias Welty, also known as Judy Goodyear and Judy Morris, was apprehended in 1984 for the murders of her husband, James Goodyear, her son, and her boyfriend, Bobby Joe Morris. She had employed a wide variety of killing methods and predominantly killed in order to secure life insurance money. Only after her execution in 1985 did police figure out that she had, in fact, committed many more murders than the three she was executed for.

Her methods of killing included poison, blowing up her boyfriend's car after trying to poison him unsuccessfully, and drowning her own son who had become disabled after she had attempted to poison him.

Q: Who was The Old Lady Killer?

Juana Barraza was arrested in 2006. She was a Mexican professional wrestler and is believed to have murdered between 42 and 48 elderly women. She would gain entry into her victims' homes by posing as a social worker and then proceed to beat the women to death and rob them. One of the things that allowed Barraza to get away with her crimes for so long is that police always believed they should be looking for a man. Despite many witnesses describing a woman leaving the homes of victims just before they were discovered as deceased, because Barraza had a very muscular build, it was assumed that the perpetrator was actually a man dressed up as a woman. As a result, the local transgender sex worker community was harassed for months on end with several arrests being made which ended in nothing.

Image 10: Female wrestlers

Barraza would eventually be apprehended when she was leaving one of her victims' homes, and her fingerprints tied her to all of the murders. She admitted to only four of the murders but could not explain the forensic links to the other scenes.

As part of her defense, Barraza alleged that it had been her mother's treatment of her as a child that had motivated her to kill. She claimed that her alcoholic mother had "sold" her to a man in exchange for three beers, and the man had raped her. She said that each time she murdered an older woman, she felt as though she was getting revenge against her mother.

Q: Which female serial killer was suspected of killing hundreds of babies?

Amelia Dyer was a British serial killer who was born in 1836 and died in prison in 1896. Although she would only be officially convicted of one murder, Dyer was believed to have killed up to 400 babies. Dyer was trained as a nurse, and after her husband died in 1869, she turned her homestead into a baby farm. Baby farming is essentially the concept of adopting unwanted children in order to gain money from the government or adoption agencies. It is said that Dyer initially did a decent job of raising the children she adopted, but soon, two of the children died and she was convicted of negligence. It is not known whether these first two deaths were intentional or not, but after she had served her six-month sentence of hard labor, something changed within Dyer, and she began to murder the children in her care. Most of the murders she committed were by strangling, and when one of her victims was found floating in the Thames river, she was arrested.

Dyer had been committed to institutions several times throughout her life, and she undoubtedly suffered from some form of mental illness. Whether this mental illness actually contributed to her murders, though, is debatable. More probable is that Dyer had been angered by her conviction for the first two deaths and decided that caring for the children was just too much trouble. At that time, there was very little oversight by any agency after a child was adopted, and it would have been relatively easy for Dyer to adopt babies, kill them, and still receive monthly payment for their care without anyone figuring out anything was wrong for quite some time.

Another interesting fact about Amelia Dyer is that she was active around the same time as infamous serial killer Jack the Ripper. After her arrest and the truth of her horrific actions came out, she was briefly considered as a possible suspect in the Jack the Ripper slayings.

Q: Which female serial killer is known as The Angel of Death?

As we've previously discussed, it is very common to find serial killers in the healthcare industry. Their crimes will often go undetected for long periods as they will generally choose victims who are quite ill anyway and kill them in ways that emulate a natural death. As these deaths generally occur in hospitals or other healthcare facilities, they are often not investigated as anything other than the natural deaths that they resemble.

Kristen Gilbert was one such murderous healthcare worker. The woman who would become known as The Angel of Death qualified as a nurse in 1988. It is sadly also not uncommon for serial killers in the healthcare industry to be allowed to continue with their crimes because, even when questions start being asked, as long as the person in question resigns from a facility, the hospital will hardly ever take further action or launch a major investigation. More often, the serial killer simply moves on to another facility and continues to kill.

Although this is not exactly what happened with Kristen when she started her career at Veterans Affairs Medical Center in 1989, other nurses soon started to notice the high death toll on her ward when she worked. This was when the name "Angel of Death" was coined by her coworkers, and it was actually done in a joking manner because no one for a minute believed that the high death rate was anything more than a coincidence. Soon though, three nurses became concerned that perhaps the high number of deaths was more than a coincidence as they realized that most deaths on Kristen's shift were cardiac related, and there was also a decrease in the supply levels of the drug epinephrine. Epinephrine is also known as adrenaline, and it is used to help increase heart rate in patients with a low heart rate.

An investigation was launched into the deaths, and Kristen resigned and booked herself into seven mental health facilities during the next three months. The investigation revealed that Kristen could have been responsible for up to 350 deaths as well as more than 300 medical emergencies in which the patients survived. She would inject epinephrine into patients to induce cardiac arrest and then attend to the emergency herself. Many believed that she had done so to get the attention of her boyfriend who also worked at the hospital.

Kristen would eventually be convicted of only four murders and sentenced to four life terms.

Q: Are there any female serial killers who have killed their own children?

Despite some of the heinous crimes that are committed by serial killers, taking the lives of one's own offspring still seems to rank way up there on the scale of evil. The act itself seems to go against everything we believe the parent-child relationship to represent. While it is bad enough when a male serial killer kills his own child, which has been seen in some sexually motivated crimes, it somehow seems worse when a mother kills her own children.

Martha Ann Johnson first got married at the age of 14. By the time she was 22, she had been married three times. She had children with each of her husbands including a baby girl from her first marriage who was born in 1971, a son in 1975 from her second marriage, and another son and daughter from her third marriage born in 1979 and 1980.

In 1977, her son from her second marriage, who was by then almost two years old, passed away after Martha claimed that he had suddenly stopped breathing in his sleep. His death was attributed to Sudden Infant Death Syndrome (SIDS). Today, while SIDS is still a determination used for many unexplained child deaths, most doctors will not allocate this prognosis to a child older than 12 months.

In 1980, just three months after her daughter was born, Martha claimed to have found the child blue and motionless in her crib. Paramedics were unable to revive her, and she passed away.

In 1989, her youngest son also stopped breathing. The child was rushed to the hospital and was kept alive on machines for several days until he was declared brain dead, and the machines were switched off.

Martha's oldest daughter, who had been exposed to the deaths of three of her siblings, would speak of nightmares that she had about her mother suffocating her. Just a year after her youngest brother's death, 11-year-old Jennyann was found lifeless, face down on her bed with foam coming out of her mouth.

After Jennyann's death, an investigation was launched which would eventually lead to a confession by Martha. She claimed, though, that she had only been responsible for the last two deaths and not for the first two. She would eventually be found guilty in a court of law for killing the last two children, and although she was initially sentenced to death, this would be commuted to a life sentence.

It emerged that 250-pound Martha had killed her children by laying her full weight on top of them until they stopped breathing. The investigation would also show that each murder coincided with an argument with one of her husbands.

Although Martha is certainly classified as a serial killer, her particular crimes are quite different from what we might see in other killers, as she seemed to only be a danger to her own children. She had been in the company of many other children throughout the years and had made no attempt to harm them. By the time she married her fourth husband, shortly before she was convicted, medical professionals confirmed that she was no longer able to become pregnant and would never again bear her own offspring.

Q: Which pediatric nurse was also a serial killer?

Genene Anne Jones qualified as a pediatric nurse in the late 1970s. It soon became apparent that an inordinate number of children were going into distress and dying while she was on shift.

Jones worked as a licensed vocational nurse, which is different to a registered nurse in that the former undertakes a less formal training program than the latter. When the hospital that Jones started her career at realized that there was likely something untoward happening with the woman and her patients, they were concerned that they were going to be sued. Instead of launching an investigation, they fired all of their licensed vocational nurses, including Jones, and replaced them with registered nurses. Jones moved on to another healthcare facility. It was at this facility, a pediatric clinic in Kerrville, Texas, that she would eventually be investigated for administering poison to the children in her care. She was charged with the murders of six children, who she was alleged to have killed by injecting them with an anesthetic agent which stopped their breathing. Jones was eventually convicted of killing two children in her care.

In 2017, though, when it became clear that Jones may well soon be released from prison, the District Attorney laid further charges against her for another five deaths. She eventually pleaded guilty to one of the cases on the condition that the other four charges would be dropped. For this crime she was sentenced to life in prison and will only be eligible for parole when she is 87 years old.

The motive behind Jones's crimes was never fully revealed, but in looking back at her life, it appears that the murders coincided with problems she was experiencing in her romantic life.

Q: Which female serial killer only served one year in prison?

Mary Clement was a serial killer in the late 1880s who killed her parents and two sisters by poisoning them. The deaths of her family members were not immediately thought to be suspicious, as she had spaced out the deaths over five years. After the murder of her father in 1885, Mary then went to live with the family of her only surviving sister.

Soon after Mary's arrival in her sister's home, that family too began to feel ill after each meal that Mary had prepared for them. She would be charged with attempting to kill them after her brother-in-law found a bag of poison on the property and then spotted the residue of that same poison in his meal.

Mary Clement was sentenced to one year in prison as, in her trial, she successfully raised doubts about her sister's reasons for accusing her. Many of those who knew Mary believed that she was innocent, but while imprisoned, she wrote a letter in which she confessed to attempting to poison her sister's family and also to killing her parents and two other siblings.

Despite this confession, she was released after she had served her sentence and not charged with any of the other crimes. It is believed that after being released from prison, she went on to live a normal life and never killed again. She died at the age of 81 from natural causes.

CHAPTER 6
SERIAL KILLERS ACROSS THE GLOBE

Although most of the more infamous serial killers are American, and the United States has the highest number of serial killers of any country in the world, there are certainly other countries in the world from which some heinous killers have emerged.

The country with the second highest number of serial killers is the United Kingdom, and the third highest is South Africa. Interestingly, although serial killers are mostly the same across the globe, they do seem to differ slightly in the modus operandi and victim selection criteria depending on their region of origin.

Many researchers believe that although there is data to support the ranking of countries based on the number of serial killers, it is important to remember that there are other factors that play a role in these numbers as well. The way in which law enforcement is set up in a specific country also plays a major role in how numbers are recorded and even how many serial killers are apprehended. A country like the United States which has many different law enforcement agencies that are not always connected and don't always share information may actually have higher numbers than they think. Countries like the United Kingdom and South Africa have connected agencies throughout their country and share information. This makes it easier to figure out when a serial killer is at work, and, therefore, their apprehension statistics may be higher than elsewhere.

In South Africa, for instance, a serial killer is usually apprehended within six to eight weeks of a series being identified, whereas in other parts of the world, this can take anywhere from three months to a year, or even longer. The set-up of law enforcement in South Africa is one reason for this, but that country's expertise in catching serial killers is also a bit of a chicken and egg situation. After the end of Apartheid, the country found itself in a very unique position. Non-White South Africans who had previously been forced to live in segregated areas were now free to move around to find better places to live and to seek employment. This sudden surge of people into urban areas meant that those with nefarious intentions were now free to move as they pleased. It also meant that they now had a far larger pool of victims who were far from home and not in constant contact with their families. If someone went missing, it would take far longer for their families to notice. Another contributing factor was that the South African police were in the process of a transition. The non-White people that they were previously tasked with controlling and suppressing now equally qualified for their protection along with White South Africans, and it took some time for this transition to be affected.

This convergence of circumstances, along with the poor socioeconomic conditions that many South Africans grew up in, resulted in an explosion of serial killers in that country in the 1990s. Authorities had no choice but to take this new criminal threat seriously and would go on to develop one of the most highly skilled investigative psychology and profiling units in the world.

The influence of socioeconomic circumstances on the development of serial killers and the ferocity of their crimes is an interesting factor to take into account when we consider serial crimes across the world. In most cases, the most vicious and prolific killers come from countries with poor socioeconomic circumstances. There is always the outlier, though, and if we consider that one of the most heartless and arguably the most prolific serial killers of all time, Dr. Harold Shipman, is British, this theory seems to go out the window. In this chapter, we take a look at some of the worst international serial killers in history.

Q: Which Columbian serial killer was nicknamed *The Beast*?

In 1999, Luis Garavito confessed to having murdered 147 young boys after raping and torturing them. One hundred thirty-eight of these murders were confirmed, and in order to return the remains to the families, prosecutors reached a deal with the horrendous killer that he would be considered for parole. Garavito was sentenced to 1,853 years in prison, but Columbian law only allows for a maximum sentence of 30 years, so, frighteningly, Garavito will be considered for parole in 2029.

Image 11: Homeless child

Garavito earned his nickname, The Beast, because of the particularly savage nature of his crimes. He would lure children from poor backgrounds with the promise of sweets, gifts, and cash, and after killing the children, he would dismember them and dispose of their bodies. Many of Garavito's victims have never been found, and once police started comparing his movements and modus operandi to reports of missing children, they estimated that his victim count may have been close to 300.

Q: Is there a serial killer that kills serial killers?

No, really, the truth is stranger than fiction. Technically, Pedro Filho hasn't killed any serial killers yet, but that is only because no one in his home country of Brazil has exceeded his body count yet.

Pedro Filho was convicted of 71 murders in 2003. He had been in and out of prison for most of his life, and by the time he was 18, he had already killed 10 people. Filho's high body count can be attributed to the fact that being imprisoned did not stop him from killing. Forty-seven of his victims were fellow inmates.

It is alleged that Filho's problems started while he was still in the womb as his alcoholic father had beaten his mother, and Filho received a head injury before he was even born. His childhood was no better, and he would eventually end up making his father one of his victims.

It is believed that Filho may be responsible for up to 100 murders. He is now imprisoned in isolation for the protection of his fellow inmates.

Q: Who is China's Family Serial Killer?

Yang Xinhai is believed to have killed up to 300 people in a three-year span. The Chinese serial killer, who was convicted and sentenced to death in 2004, managed to achieve this prolific spree in such a short period by breaking into houses and annihilating entire families.

Xinhai used a wide range of weapons and often whatever was available to him, including shovels, axes, meat cleavers, and hammers. It is likely this flexibility that also aided in him killing so many people before he was caught. It is alleged that he was triggered to kill after breaking up with his girlfriend who he had intended to marry. He would claim that he decided that if he could not have a family then no one else would either.

Q: Why was Alexander Pichushkin called the *Chessboard Killer*?

Russia's Alexander Pichushkin is possibly one of the most chilling serial killers in history because he really seemed to see murder as a game. Pichushkin started out killing with a very specific plan. He wanted to kill exactly 68 people, one for each square on a chessboard. It is believed that he had another reason for wanting to kill that many people, and that was to surpass the body count of the most prolific serial killer in Russia at that time, the Rostov Ripper, who had killed 53 people.

Pichushkin targeted mostly homeless and elderly men, luring them with the promise of alcohol before beating them to death with a hammer. He did not reach his target of 68 victims, thankfully, and his body count is put at somewhere between 48 and 60.

Pichushkin was so hated by the public that he was held in a safety-glass cage during his trial to prevent him from being attacked. His crimes spanned from 1992 to 2006 when he was arrested, and he was sentenced to life imprisonment.

Q: Which South African serial killer had authorities believing that he was actually two separate serial killers?

In 1996, two separate series of murders presented themselves to South African police in geographical areas that were three miles apart. One profile was created for a man they called the Wemmer Pan killer, who was attacking couples walking or sitting by the lake called Wemmer Pan. He would shoot or bludgeon them to death and on one occasion used a knife. Three miles away, in the city center of Johannesburg, police were searching for a man who was killing tailors and other shopkeepers with a hammer. The man would present himself as a prospective customer and then quite suddenly strike his victim with a hammer. Most victims died before they were found by other customers. This serial killer was given the nickname *The Hammer Killer*.

Image 12: Hammer

Two separate profiles were created for the two perpetrators who were believed to have been responsible for the crimes, and the country's top serial killer investigator at the time was assigned to the case.

In 1997, Cedric Maake was arrested for the Wemmer Pan series. During investigations into his background, police uncovered a pseudonym that Maake had used. They soon realized that this was the same pseudonym that had been used by the Hammer Killer when he posed as a customer at a tailor shop before bludgeoning the owner to death. It was only then that investigators realized that they didn't have two serial killers on their hands but one single killer who was so adaptable in his methods that he presented as two different criminals.

There were so many differences in modus operandi, victim selection, and method of killing between these two series that even seasoned detectives who had worked on countless serial killer investigations before were convinced they had two perpetrators on their hands.

Every now and then, a serial killer emerges that is completely different from anything we have ever seen, and Cedric Maake proved that we don't perhaps know as much as we think we do.

Q: Which serial killer was sentenced to die in the same way he had killed his victims?

Every country has its own justice system, and just as the death sentence is not legal in all states in America, it is also not legal in all countries in the world. Everyone also has their own idea of what justice really means. For some, incarceration for life when a killer has taken the lives of countless innocent victims is simply not enough. Some feel that allowing a serial killer to live out their days with free lodging, food, and medical care is a slap in the face to those who lost their lives. In Pakistan, the death sentence is still imposed for the most serious of crimes, and the courts have the authority to impose any form of death penalty they see fit. While most death sentences in Pakistan are carried out by firing squad, in one specific serial killer's case, the courts felt a more severe penalty was in order.

Javed Iqbal walked into the offices of a Pakistani newspaper in 1999. He confessed to murdering 100 young boys and said that he was handing himself in because he feared for his life. He claimed that Pakistani police would kill him if he surrendered to them, so he was alerting newspaper staff to save his own life. Iqbal was arrested and it emerged that the man was indeed the deranged killer of 100 children. Most of his victims were runaways or indigent children, and he had raped, strangled, and dismembered his victims before dissolving their remains in hydrochloric acid. When police searched Iqbal's home, they found the partially dissolved remains of some victims there.

After being found guilty, Iqbal was sentenced to death. The judge decreed that Iqbal would be hanged in front of his victims' families and then his body would be dismembered and dissolved in acid in the same way he had done to his victims. This, the judge felt, would be true justice. Iqbal, though, was not going to allow this to be done, and just days before his execution was to be carried out, he committed suicide by hanging himself in his prison cell. Right to the end, the deranged criminal insisted on maintaining control.

Q: Which French serial killer used World War II to lure his victims?

Serial killers by their very nature are cunning and manipulative and will often use events and situations that are happening in their surroundings to lure victims. Many South African serial killers, for instance, use the fact that the country has a high unemployment rate to deceive victims into believing they have job opportunities available for them, only to attack and kill them. Many of the international serial killers we have looked at so far, living in poorer countries, lured their victims by taking advantage of their desperation. One French serial killer, though, took this to a completely different level of evil. Marcel Petiot was a medical doctor, but he didn't commit his crimes in the way most deadly doctors do. Instead, he used his standing in society to lull people into a false sense of security. During World War II, when most Jewish people were fleeing for their lives, Petiot invited these people into his home. He pretended that his home was a safe haven for those running from the Nazis, but instead, he killed those he had claimed to be protecting.

He is believed to have killed over 60 people, although he was only convicted of killing 23. He would kill them by administering a lethal injection which he claimed was a vaccine against local diseases. He would then keep the bodies in his basement and burn them in a specially built fireplace. It was this method of disposal that would eventually be his undoing, as neighbors complained to the police about the foul-smelling smoke coming from Petiot's home.

Petiot fled from police for some time but was eventually arrested and found guilty of 23 murders. He claimed that he had only been attempting to help the war effort by killing enemies of the state. Petiot was executed by guillotine in 1946.

Q: Which Russian policeman became a serial killer?

Mikhail Popkov is a Russian serial killer who holds many records. Not only was he a trusted member of law enforcement in that country who betrayed his oath to protect and serve by instead raping and killing, but he also killed over two decades and had a geographical span of almost 2,500 miles. Popkov's crimes were so vicious that he was given the moniker *The Werewolf* because his victims looked like they had been attacked by wild animals by the time he was finished with them. He was also quite different in the various methods of killing he used, including axes, baseball bats, screwdrivers, and knives. There is no doubt that by breaking all the rules of how serial killers are "supposed" to behave, Popkov bought himself much more time to kill before he was caught.

His background in law enforcement also likely served him well as it would have been relatively easy for him to know what was happening with the investigation of his own murders. He would have also known how to dispose of evidence effectively to avoid being detected.

Popkov was initially arrested, tried, and found guilty of 22 murders in 2015. In 2018, he confessed to another 59 murders. He was found guilty of 56 of those. Popkov admitted to using his police uniform to fool his victims into believing they were in a safe situation before he brutally murdered them.

Q: Who is Japan's *Black Widow* serial killer?

The female black widow spider is known for killing its partners after mating. The term black widow has been used over the years to describe women who behave in the same way. One such Japanese woman, Chisako Kakehi, was sentenced to death in 2017 at the age of 72 for having killed at least four of her partners. Kakehi cold-bloodedly selected her victims based on whether they were wealthy and whether they had children. The latter criterion was to ensure that she would inherit all of their estate when they died. She is believed to have targeted at least 14 men and many of these died, but only four could be proven as murder because some of the other bodies were cremated without autopsy.

Her chosen method of killing was cyanide, which she discovered through her first husband who ran a printing company as small amounts of cyanide were used in the printing process. This husband died in 1994 after having been discharged from the hospital after recovering from a heart attack. Her second husband died in 2006, allegedly of a stroke. The very next year, Kakehi became engaged to a 79-year-old man who had cancer. He suddenly collapsed soon after they had become engaged and remained on life support for two years. Traces of cyanide were found in his system.

In 2008, Kakehi married her third husband, and he died just three months after marrying her, apparently from a heart attack. In 2011, Kakehi's latest fiancé also died. In 2013, a man she was dating died soon after having dinner with her.

Eventually, in 2014, police investigated the death of Kakehi's fourth husband, who died just a month after they got married. She was found to have poisoned him with cyanide, and she was arrested. During the investigation into this case, the trail of dead partners Kakehi had left behind came to light. Her main motivation was believed to be large life insurance policies that these men had left for her.

CHAPTER 7
LESSER-KNOWN SERIAL KILLERS

In the world of serial killers, there are the names that everyone associates with serial murder—Ted Bundy, Jeffrey Dahmer, Jack the Ripper—and there are those who somehow slip by undetected by the mass media. Perhaps their capture coincides with another major event, or their crimes are seen as less newsworthy. Sometimes serial killers are only identified as such after they have been in prison on other charges for some time. One by one, more cases are revealed, and someone who may have only been arrested for one murder is eventually found to be a pretty prolific serial killer. In this chapter, we will dive deep down into the annals of true crime history and dig out some of the most obscure and certainly less infamous serial killers of all time.

Q: Which serial killer sold the baby of one of his victims?

John Robinson is one of those serial killers who didn't just manage to stay under the radar of law enforcement for decades, but he somehow also managed to avoid the spotlight of the media. Robinson is possibly one of the most heartless killers I've come across as he preyed on women who were experiencing difficulties in their lives and offered them assistance only to brutally rape and kill them. Among his victims were a mother and disabled daughter who he murdered and stored in barrels in his basement. He collected the pair's disability checks from the government for years after their death.

Image 13: Baby

Robinson was not just a vicious killer but also a prolific con man. He held very few honest jobs in his life despite having a wife and four children, and most of the employment he got or money he made was as a result of lies and deceit. He was so good at lying that he even managed to con a doctor into believing that he was a qualified radiologist. One of Robinson's many schemes involved setting up a fake charity which he claimed assisted unwed mothers in crisis. He used this ruse to lure one of his first victims who he killed while her infant child was in the same room. He then sold her baby to his brother and sister-in-law, claiming it was a legal adoption, and charged them $5,500. The couple believed for almost 16 years that they were raising a legally adopted child only to find out after Robinson's arrest that she was in fact the result of one of his crimes.

Despite being linked to over 11 murders, he would only be convicted of three, but he was still sentenced to death. Robinson continues to claim that he is innocent. Possibly one of the reasons his crimes have remained lesser known is that any journalist or writer who approaches him for comments or to provide information about his history is met with demands for ludicrous amounts of money. Robinson demanded $400,000 from one author who simply wanted to include some information about him in a single chapter of a book he was writing. The serial killer may be locked away, but the con man is still alive and well it seems.

Q: Which serial killer left a deathbed confession to 21 murders with his attorney?

It is believed that Larry Eyler started killing in his early 30s. He would lure male victims by pretending that they were going to have consensual sex and then handcuff and beat them to death. He got his nickname, The Highway Killer, from dumping his victims on the side of highways. Police realized pretty quickly that they had a serial killer on their hands when all of the victims were found with their pants around their ankles and disemboweled.

Eyler was eventually caught after he left a tire track at one of the scenes. Police put him under surveillance and saw him dumping trash bags in a dumpster nowhere near his home. When the bags were retrieved, they were found to contain the remains of a 15-year-old boy who was his latest victim. During the sentencing phase of Eyler's trial, he tried to make a deal with the prosecutor by saying that he would confess to 21 additional murders if the death penalty was taken off the table. The deal was rejected, and Eyler was sentenced to die by lethal injection.

In 1994, Eyler died of AIDS-related complications before his execution could be carried out. Upon his death, his attorney handed over 21 confessions that Eyler had left with him, to be released upon his death.

Police were able to line up these confessions with the physical evidence at the scenes of these crimes, and all 21 cases were attributed to Eyler and closed.

Q: Which serial killer sent letters and hand-drawn maps to the police indicating where his victims could be found?

Peter Kurten was a German serial killer who committed over 30 murders beginning in the summer of 1929. He would send the police letters written in a friendly tone in which he expressed his desire to kill as many people as people, and each letter was accompanied by a hand-drawn map leading police to his latest victim. Kurten preferred to kill young women, but his victims also included men and children. He became known as the Vampire of Dusseldorf when, after his arrest, he admitted that he would drink blood from the necks of his victims. Kurten was sentenced to death by guillotine in 1931.

Q: Which serial killer only became one after being released from jail for killing children?

Arthur Shawcross is best known for killing 11 sex workers between March 1988 and January 1990. Although this was Shawcross's longest undisturbed series, this was not the first time the man had killed someone. Shawcross would claim that his first two murders occurred when he served in the army in Vietnam. He said that he had killed and cannibalized two Vietnamese women during his enlistment. These claims have never been proved, but we do know that Shawcross was imprisoned in 1972 for killing a 10-year-old boy and an 8-year-old girl. A plea bargain managed to get this self-confessed child killer 25 years in prison, and he served only 15.

In a similar way to how a serial rapist may get out of prison and decide to start killing his rape victims to silence them, when Shawcross was released from jail, he had decided to change tack in his victim selection to avoid detection. Seemingly realizing that children were high-profile victims that were difficult to get his hands on and that police would launch intensive manhunts to find a child killer, he decided to start taking less conspicuous victims. Shawcross undoubtedly knew that sex workers would be far more available victims, and also less likely to be noticed as missing within a short period. This major shift in victim typology is extremely rare and points to the possibility that Shawcross was not as driven by a specific fantasy as some other serial killers.

Q: Which serial killer killed across five continents?

Carl Panzram's name barely registers on the list of serial killers probably because he was active in the 1920s, but he is probably the only serial killer who killed across multiple continents. Panzram had been in and out of prison for most of his life for various offences, and he claimed to have been the victim of many violent prison beatings which had left him filled with hate. He started his murders in New York where he killed several adult males and two small children. He then launched into living a nomadic lifestyle in which he killed in Scotland, South America, Europe, and Africa. When he was eventually arrested, he told police that his only regret was being born.

Q: Which British serial killer's surviving victims wished that he had succeeded in killing them?

In 1975, the women in a small British town were terrified when it became clear that a serial killer was haunting their streets. By the time the man known as The Ripper was caught, he had killed 13 women and left 7 more barely clinging to life. The man, who would later be identified as Peter Sutcliffe, would strike his victims over the head with a hammer and then slash their stomachs open with a knife.

Image 14: Knife

After his arrest, his seven surviving victims testified against him in court, and their testimony around the psychological, emotional, and physical scars they endured was horrific. Some even testified that their suffering was still so great many years after their encounter with The Ripper, that they didn't feel very lucky to have survived.

Q: Who is the serial killer that killed his victims for companionship?

Scottish serial killer Dennis Nilsen killed 15 men over the period of five years while living in London. What made his crimes and the fact that he isn't more well-known strange is that Nilsen claimed to kill only because he was lonely.

After a string of failed relationships, Nilsen allegedly decided that no partner would ever leave him again, and he made sure of this by killing every man he brought home. Nilsen would go out to local bars and pick up men and bring them home. He would have sexual encounters with these men and invite them to sleep over. Once they were asleep, Nilsen would kill the men. Bizarrely, he would keep the body with him for as long as he could, treating it like a live person. He would talk to the bodies, bathe them, seat them at the table with him while he ate, and watch dinner with them. When the bodies became too decomposed to keep, he would dismember them, and flush the pieces down the toilet.

It was this misguided method of disposal which would be Nilsen's undoing, as in 1983, a plumber working in the apartment building he lived in found pieces of human flesh in the drains, and the police were called. After an extensive search of every apartment, police soon narrowed down the source of the body parts, and Nilsen was arrested and sentenced to life in prison.

Q: Which serial killer stored his victims' teeth in his mother's attic?

Gerald Schaefer, who was active in Florida in 1973, should be far more infamous than he is. Schaefer would only be convicted of killing two women, but he is positively linked to more than 30 murders. Schaefer should also be infamous for several other shocking reasons, including the fact that he was an active police officer while he was committing his crimes. He would often kidnap a woman, tie her to a tree, and then go off to finish his shift as a policeman. After he finished his shift, he would return to his victim and rape, torture, mutilate, and murder them.

After his arrest, it was found that he was storing trophies from his murders, including teeth that he had extracted during his torture sessions, in a trunk in his mother's attic.

Q: Who is the Vancouver Child Killer?

Westley Allan Dodd had a pretty normal childhood. He doesn't report having been molested or physically or emotionally abused in any way. Despite this, as many pedophiles secretly do, he began exposing himself to young children when he was just 13 years old. He then soon moved on to molestation, and in 1989, he killed for the first time. By the time he was arrested, he had killed three children and attempted to kidnap his fourth victim.

Dodd would be dubbed the Vancouver Child Killer and was allegedly so repulsed by his own actions that he asked to be hanged in 1993. Whether his request was really due to his disgust in his actions or had more to do with the fact that child killers are notoriously unpopular in prison remains to be seen.

Q: Which serial killer kept a scorecard in the trunk of his car to record his victims?

In 1983, Randy Steven Kraft was arrested after being linked to the torture, rape, mutilation, and murder of 16 young men. He would pick his victims up as they walked on freeways in California. When he was arrested, a search of his vehicle revealed a scorecard hidden in the trunk of his car. Kraft, it seemed, had been recording each and every one of the murders he committed for posterity. His scorecard system revealed that he may have had more than 50 victims, although the validity of this could not be confirmed. He received the moniker *The Scorecard Killer* in the media when this fact was revealed in his trial.

Kraft was sentenced to death and remains on death row to this day.

Q: Which lesser-known serial killer is a legend in the forensic science community?

Faryion Wardrip is not a name that is uttered regularly when serial killers are discussed, but for forensic scientists, his case represents a turning point in DNA investigation.

Wardrip was placed under surveillance for some time before he was arrested in order to gather enough evidence to make charges of murder stick. Police suspected that he was the killer of five women that had recently been found murdered in quick succession. Up until this point in investigations, police had predominantly only procured DNA from warranted seizures, but in Wardrip's case, they had to be a little more creative.

While conducting surveillance of the man, police recognized that he was a creature of habit. Every morning before work, Wardrip would purchase a takeout coffee on his way to work. He would drink it while he drove and then dispose of the empty styrofoam cup in a trash can outside his place of work. One sharp-minded police officer wondered if there was a way that forensic scientists could extract DNA from his saliva and skin cells on that coffee cup. At this point, this type of DNA extraction was uncommon, but the police's forensic team told investigators it was worth a try.

The next time Wardrip purchased his customary takeout coffee, drank it, and disposed of it in the trash can, police were ready to pounce. After Wardrip had gone into his place of work, a plain-clothes policeman retrieved the cup with gloved hands, and it was sent off for analysis.

The attempt paid off, and the DNA from the coffee cup was a match to DNA found at some of the murder scenes. Wardrip was arrested, convicted, and sentenced to life in prison.

Q: Which serial killer was almost overlooked as a suspect due to incorrect racial profiling?

When police were hunting the Baton Rouge serial killer in 2004, inaccurate racial profiling almost allowed the real killer to get away when they focused solely on White suspects during their investigation. Despite the fact that any law enforcement should have known better by that time, investigators still operated under the assumption that most serial killers are White. This almost allowed the real serial killer, Derrick Todd Lee, an African American man, to escape capture.

Lee's modus operandi was to watch victims in their homes before he selected his victims. He started out as a serial rapist and soon escalated to murder. He was given the death sentence for his crimes but died in prison in 2014 before the sentence could be passed down.

Q: Who is Darren Vann?

In 2014, the body of a 19-year-old girl was found in a bathtub of a motel. She had been raped and strangled. CCTV from the motel easily identified her killer, and Darren Vann was soon arrested and charged with the woman's murder. What police did not know when they were arresting Vann, though, is that they were also about to solve six other murders.

After his arrest, Vann began to sing like a bird and even led police to bodies that had not yet been found as he had secreted them away in abandoned and condemned buildings. It also emerged that Vann had only just been released from prison when he had killed the woman in the motel room. In 2009, he was sent to prison on an aggravated rape charge, and he was released in July 2013. He started killing very soon after his release, with the victim in the motel room being his seventh victim in less than a year.

Q: Which serial killer called his car his "murder mobile"?

William Howell was a drifter who was convicted on a manslaughter charge in 2007. The charge emanated from the death of a young woman who was last seen getting into Howell's van in 2003. The woman's blood was found in his van, and when he was arrested, he pleaded guilty to having caused the woman's death.

Howell was known to have referred to his van as his "murder mobile," but the reason for this would only become clear much later. Shortly after Howell's arrest in 2007, three bodies were found on a desolate stretch of land behind a strip mall in Connecticut. The bodies were not immediately linked to Howell, and those murders would actually remain unsolved until 2015, when more skeletonized remains were found in the same area. The timings of the murders seemed to have coincided with Howell's activity in the area, and when investigators caught up with the man, who was still in prison on his manslaughter charge, they chatted with some of his fellow inmates. Howell, it seemed, had been rather chatty during his time in prison, and he had told several inmates about a piece of land he had used to dump many more victims that he believed police didn't know about.

The murders were positively linked to Howell, and in 2018, he was convicted of six additional murders.

Q: Who is The Shopkeeper Killer?

Salvatore Perrone was a Brooklyn business owner in his own right, until his shop started to fail, and his wife and children left him. It is alleged that this failure triggered him to start killing those who were seemingly enjoying the success he had not.

As part of his deranged plan, Salvatore put together a kill kit which he carried with him almost all the time in an innocuous looking black duffle bag. The bag contained the tools of his murderous trade including switchblades, screwdrivers, an eight-inch serrated knife, latex gloves, three women's shirts, latex gloves, wire cutters, bleach, and a sawed-off rifle. By the time police caught up with him, he had killed three shopkeepers while they were working. He was quickly convicted based on the evidence and sentenced to 75 years in prison.

Q: Which serial killer was attacked in court by the father of one of his victims?

Michael Madison was already a convicted sex offender when he moved into the East Cleveland suburb of Glenville in 2013. He had been convicted of attempted rape in 2002 and served jail time for that crime. Shortly after he moved to the area, the bodies of three young women were found wrapped in garbage bags not far from his home. Madison was quickly identified as the killer and arrested.

During his trial, he showed no remorse for his actions, and instead, displayed utter disdain for his victims' families by regularly smirking when devastating evidence of his crimes was presented. His attitude irked the father of one victim so badly that the man launched himself across the courtroom and began to beat Madison before bailiffs pulled him off.

Q: Which lesser-known serial killer allegedly went dormant for 14 years?

Lonnie David Franklin, Junior, is alleged to have started killing in 1985, continuing through 1988, and then taking a break between 1988 and 2002, when he started killing again. This sort of dormancy period is highly unlikely with serial killers and earned Franklin the moniker *The Grim Sleeper.*

Franklin specifically selected victims who would not be on the media's radar in the hopes that his murders would not be linked. His victims included drug addicts and sex workers. He would leave his victims' naked bodies on the side of the road or in alleys. Franklin was initially convicted of killing 10 women, but officials warn that this certainly may not be his real body count. During a search of his home, police seized numerous photographs of naked women who appeared to be dead. None of the photographs matched the existing victims that he was convicted for which leads police to believe that these women may have been additional victims that he killed during his so-called dormancy period.

The Grim Sleeper, it seems, may not have been "sleeping" at all.

CHAPTER 8
UNSOLVED SERIAL KILLER CASES

The only thing that is possibly more frightening than a serial killer is one that is still on the loose. We know that serial killers do not stop killing unless they die or they are arrested, so what happens when decades go by, and there is no resolution to a string of clearly linked crimes? Where do these vicious killers go when they seemingly disappear into thin air? In such cases, the best possible option is that the perpetrator has died. At least then they are no longer a threat to society. Even that option leaves a lot to be desired, though, as there are still victims' families out there who want answers and closure, and if the perpetrator dies, that closure is likely never going to come. One of the other options is that the perpetrator could be in jail for a single murder or a completely different offence. If there is DNA available in a case, then the DNA taken from the perpetrator upon their incarceration should match up. We know, though, that, especially with the older cold cases, police departments don't always have the resources to run down these leads.

As our forensic tools improve, and we develop new technology, though, there is renewed hope for cold serial cases. One such development is genetic genealogy, which helped to finally identify the Golden State Killer after so many decades of that series remaining unsolved. The more that cases like those are solved, we can only hope that there are many serial killers out there who realize that their time is coming too.

In this chapter we will take a look at the multitude of serial murder cases that remain unsolved to this day.

Q: Is Jack the Ripper the first unsolved serial killer case?

The answer to this question may be both yes and no. There is a still unsolved series of murders which occurred in Austin, Texas, that predates the Jack the Ripper killings in Whitechapel, London, but may in fact be linked.

Three years before the phantom of Jack the Ripper would start his (or her) murders in Whitechapel, London, quite a distance away in Austin, Texas, an unknown killer started to kill African American servant women. While the exact number of women killed in this series is unknown, the killer ended it by switching up his victim selection and killing two high-society ladies. He then completely disappeared. Three years later, women in Whitechapel were being slaughtered in the street by an unidentified man.

The possible link between these two unsolved series is that one of the suspects identified in the Austin murders was found to have illegally boarded a ship soon after police started asking questions. You've likely already guessed the destination of that ship—Whitechapel. Without police in Whitechapel knowing anything about this person's past in the United States, he was also looked into as a Jack the Ripper suspect. Coincidence? Perhaps, but either way, the man has never been named, nor was he arrested.

Q: Who killed 11 people at Ann Arbor Hospital?

In 1975 in Michigan, an Ann Arbor hospital was suddenly struck with a string of unexplained deaths. Patients, who although ill were not considered at imminent risk of death, started to develop breathing problems. Twenty-seven such cases would be identified, and of those cases, 11 patients died as a direct result of the sudden breathing difficulties.

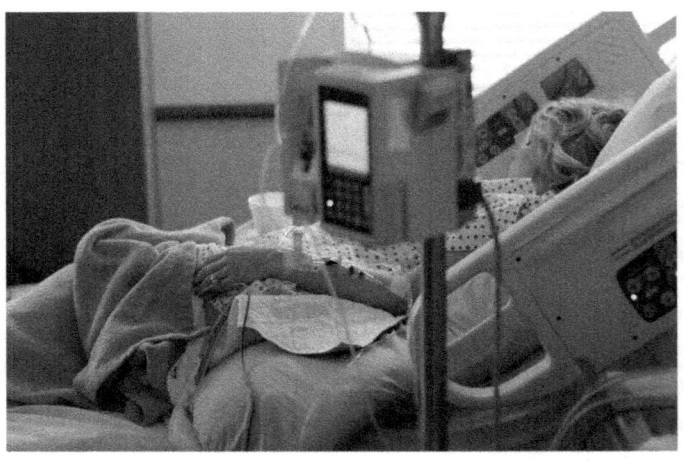

Image 15: Hospital

An investigation was launched into the seemingly inexplicable deaths. No puncture wounds were found in the bodies of the victims, but autopsies determined that 18 of those patients that had experienced breathing difficulties, including those that had died, had all ingested a drug called Pavulon. The drug is commonly used as a muscle relaxant by anesthesiologists and in big enough doses would certainly cause breathing difficulties.

The only problem was that none of the patients had been prescribed Pavulon.

The lack of puncture wounds on the victims indicated that the drug must have been administered into their feeding tubes. This, as well as the fact that the drug was not easy to procure, made investigators believe that the killer must be one of the hospital staff. The next step for investigators was to check work rosters to determine which staff members had been working shifts when victims had been administered the medication. Two Filipino nurses, Leonora Perez and Filipina Narciso, were determined to be the most likely suspects. The two women denied any involvement in the murders, but they were brought up before a grand jury and indicted. The trial proved beyond a shadow of a doubt that the victims had indeed died of an intentional overdose of Pavulon, but linking the two women to the deeds was not as easy. Surviving victims gave testimony that was confused and often changed, and it seemed to many present that these people that had been very ill at the time of the events or still ill at the time of the trial were not the most convincing of witnesses. Despite this, Perez and Narciso were found guilty of five of the murders in 1977. The very next year, though, on appeal, the flimsy convictions were overturned, and the women walked free.

The prosecution was given the opportunity to retry them but dropped the case. No further suspects have ever been identified in the murder of 11 people at this Ann Arbor Hospital, and the case remains unsolved.

Q: Was Wayne Williams really the Atlanta Child Killer?

Between 1979 and 1981 in Atlanta, Georgia, African American children were being hunted and murdered. Twenty-nine children were murdered during this period, and, although initially police attempted to relay fears by claiming that they were all individual murders, it soon became clear that there was a serial killer in Georgia.

Police would eventually arrest a man called Wayne Williams, and although they were only able to convict him of two of the murders, police insinuated that he was the killer of 22 of the other children too. Both at the time of the trial, and over the years, many have had their doubts as to whether Williams really was the serial killer they were looking for, and even if he killed anyone at all.

Image 16: Child being led away

In 2005, one such believer in Williams's innocence, a police chief in Atlanta called Louis Graham, took the major step of reopening five of the cases which occurred in his jurisdiction of East Atlanta. Graham had actually worked on some of the cases when they had originally happened as he was first starting out in the police force, and his feeling had always been that Williams was simply not the type to have committed the long string of horrendous murders. Authorities at the time had been under huge pressure to make an arrest, though, as the public started to question why police were not paying the same amount of attention to the murder of African American children as they would if the children were White.

The case that was built around Williams predominantly surrounded his activities at a community radio station and also as an aspiring music promoter. Williams owned a police scanner, and he often listened for interesting cases to be reported on the scanner and then headed over to the scene so that he could report it for the community radio station. This, police said, proved that he was involved in the cases, as they took this to be an attempt to insert himself into their investigations. The fact that Williams often had occasion to interact with young boys when they auditioned for him in his music promotion role became the second factor that made police sure he was their man. Unfortunately for the police's theory, many of the young victims' kidnappings had been witnessed, and several people reported seeing a White male in a blue Buick. Williams was an African American male, and he did not drive a blue Buick.

Sadly, many of the children who would eventually become known as victims of the Atlanta Child Killer were simply believed by police to have run away until their badly decomposed bodies were found months later.

There were several other suspects that would have been a better fit than Williams as the serial killer, but most were dismissed by police, off hand. One such suspect was convicted pedophile John Wilcoxen. The man lived in the area that the victims were disappearing from, and he could be linked to one victim directly in that the child had visited his home. The man also lived across the road from a public swimming pool that one victim had last been seen leaving. Despite Wilcoxen's known predilection for child pornography, police believed that the man would not have targeted the child because all of his prior victims had been White boys, and the deceased victim was African American. Many other cases included clues and even a telephone call from a White man who directed police to the latest victim.

Although at the time, 29 murders were attributed to the Atlanta Child Killer, a later investigation would show that there were many more murders that had not been added to the list for various reasons. The actual count of child murder with similarities in the same geographical area during that time was 63, and many of them happened after Wayne Williams was arrested.

Those who believe in Williams's innocence continue to investigate the cases that were included in this series, if not to prove that he didn't do it, then at least to find out who really did.

Q: Where did the Lovers' Lane Killer go?

Also in Atlanta, but this time, a little earlier than the child killings started, couples were being hunted in 1977. In a style similar to the Son of Sam murders, an unidentified man started his rampage by killing a couple who were making love in the back seat of their car in a park. The male victim lived long enough to climb into the driver's seat of the car and speed out of the park, but having been shot four times, he didn't not make it very far before passing away. At the same park, the next month, another couple had six shots fired into their vehicle by an unknown assailant. These victims survived and were able to identify their attacker as a tall and well-built African American man. The same caliber of bullet was used in both attacks.

The third attack occurred almost exactly a month later, again in the same park. This time, the female victim died and the male survived.

The police realized that there was almost exactly a month between the attacks, and the next month, they staked out the park, hoping to catch their killer red handed. He did not appear and never killed in Atlanta again.

Police have acknowledged that they have no leads in any of the cases, and they remain unsolved to this day.

Q: When did Chicago have four serial killers operating in one year?

In 1999, police in Chicago put out an alert to all sex workers that four different serial killers were operating in the city at that time. Twelve murdered sex workers had been found in the past few months in Chicago, and DNA testing had determined that four different men were responsible for the murders. The murders seemed to be centered around a very specific area, and it was believed that all four serial killers were focusing on crack-addicted sex workers in the area who were likely desperate to work and would go with someone even if their gut told them otherwise.

The modus operandi of all four killers was extremely similar, and all of the victims were found in abandoned buildings in the area. The decrepit nature of the buildings and their hidden entrances made police believe that the killers had to be picking out the locations when it was light, as it would have been almost impossible to find these places at night, if you didn't already know where they were.

Three men would eventually be arrested for a varied split of the murders, but it would be an ongoing dispute among defense attorneys about who was responsible for which murders. To this day, there are still several of the original 12 murders that are still unsolved, and very likely at least one of those serial killers is still on the loose.

Q: Which unsolved serial murder case was responsible for the tamper-proof medicine containers we have today?

In the early 1980s, seven people were killed when a still unidentified serial killer laced Tylenol capsules with cyanide and left the tampered product on store shelves for purchase. This was the first time that police had seen this method of killing, which essentially involved product tampering. Three of the victims were from the same family. As many of the deaths occurred in the same area of Chicago, a few of the victims were attended to by the same paramedic service. It would be a casual discussion between the medics that would solve the riddle as to what had linked all the sudden deaths. Many family members reported that the deceased person had taken a Tylenol capsule before collapsing.

Besides being the case that sparked the development of tamper-proof medication packaging, this case would also go on to be a marketing model on how to handle a crisis. The manufacturer of the drug, Johnson and Johnson, did such a great job in handling the recall and crisis response to the terrible events that the popularity of Tylenol hardly dropped at all. Today it remains one of the most popular nonprescription pain medications in the United States, and the deaths of seven people at the hand of one madman still remain unsolved.

Q: Who killed five homeless men in Denver and then disappeared?

In 1999 in Denver, the bodies of five homeless men were discovered within a relatively short space of time. All men had been brutally beaten to death, and all were found within a six-block radius of the city. The only thing that differentiated the murders was the manner in which the victims were beaten. Some had been struck with a weapon while others had been assaulted with the perpetrator's fists. One of the victims had been decapitated, and only his body was initially found, with his head being located several weeks later.

Police quickly realized that they had a serial killer on their hands and took steps to try and protect the city's homeless people. Shelters were allowed to take in more people than they were licensed to, and some motels started to take in the homeless. Despite all of this effort, another two victims would be found decapitated, and sadly, their heads were never located. Confusion ensued when some homeless people came forward to report having been beaten by two teenage boys. Police were sure that it was not possible that the teenage boys were responsible for the beheading murders as well, as that is more of a pathological and solitary crime. Authorities were now unsure if they had one killer who was changing his modus operandi or two separate serial killers. The killings stopped at this point, and the perpetrator has never been identified.

Q: Why are there so many unsolved serial murders centered around the interstate?

The Dwight D. Eisenhower National System of Interstate and Defense Highways is commonly known as the interstate and is a network of highways used in the United States to travel between states. With United States law enforcement being split up into different agencies, and each of those agencies focusing on a specific town, county, and state, throughout the years serial killers have learned to use this to their advantage. There have been many serial killers who, since the interstate system was built, have used it as their dumping ground. This often helps to muddy the waters when it comes to an investigation as many different agencies might become involved if victims are found in different counties and states.

Despite these difficulties, many cases of serial murder along the interstate have been successfully investigated and solved in the past. Some though remain unsolved to this day.

One such case is the I-10 serial killer. Interstate 10 is 2,500 miles long and winds through eight different states. In 1981, a woman, whose identity was protected, informed police that she knew a serial killer who was operating on the stretch of highway. She approached San Diego police with information about a murder that had taken place that year that she had witnessed. The killer, she said, was a long-distance truck driver who had, to her knowledge, killed more than 20 people on his travels. The details she provided about the murder were so accurate that police could not deny she was telling the truth. She said that the serial killer usually killed his victims in Texas and then dumped the bodies hundreds of miles away in different states to avoid detection. When San Diego police investigated, they found that law enforcement agencies along that stretch of highway had indeed had several unsolved murders cropping up, and all the victims were dumped along the I-10.

Despite a task force being set up, the murders were never solved, and the trucker was never identified.

At the same time, another interstate killer was operating, this time on the I-35 stretch of the highway. This section is considerably shorter than the I-10 at just 420 miles, but the killer managed to rack up 22 victims between 1976 and 1981.

The unidentified killer usually targeted hitchhikers or motorists experiencing problems with their vehicles. Police did not believe that this killer was a trucker as the first victim was last seen getting into a van before her body was found a few days later. She had been stabbed in the neck.

The next victims of the I-35 killer were a couple who had run out of gas and were stuck on the side of the highway. The couple's bodies were found in separate places, but both had been shot with the same weapon. In the third instance attributed to this killer, a young woman was found shot once in the abdomen along the highway. She was still alive when she was found but died in the hospital 10 days later without ever having regained consciousness. The next murder would be a stabbing of a young woman who was abducted from her broken-down vehicle.

The next victim of this killer would become one of the most well-known Jane Doe cases in modern history. On Halloween of 1979, the body of a young woman was found. She was naked except for a pair of orange socks. Police were unable to identify her despite extensive appeals to the public, and the Jane Doe became known as Orange Socks. The serial killer Henry Lee Lucas, who confessed to killing over 100 people, would take responsibility for the murder of Orange Socks, but authorities believe it is highly unlikely that he committed the murder as he was unable to provide an accurate description of the scene and what had been done to the victim.

Orange Socks was eventually identified in 2019 with the help of the DNA Doe Project and a new sketch which had been produced. The victim's surviving sister recognized the sketch and approached police. A DNA comparison showed that Orange Socks was indeed her sister. The victim's name is now known to be Debra Jackson. Although Debra was last seen by her family in 1977, she was never reported missing, and her family seemed to assume she had just built a life for herself elsewhere and did not wish to remain in contact.

Three more victims of the I-35 killer would be discovered before authorities acknowledged that they likely had a serial killer on their hands. Despite an active investigation continuing for many years, the I-35 killer has never been identified.

Some sections of the interstate are so popular with serial killers that the stretches receive nicknames to denote the frequency with which they are used as dumping grounds. One such section is I-70, which runs between Indianapolis and Ohio, and is referred to as "America's Sewer Pipe." In the late 1970s, the bodies of nine gay men were found dumped on I-7o. Despite huge publicity, the killer was never identified.

There were suspects in the I-70 killings over the years, including a businessman, Herb Baumeister, who despite being a married man with three children was known to frequent gay bars. Baumeister came to police's attention in 1993 when men began disappearing from the Indianapolis area. Ten men went missing over the span of two years, but police made no headway with locating them or the killer. Then a man came forward to say that he had visited a large estate in the area with a man he had met at a bar. The man had enjoyed autoerotic asphyxiation as part of his routine sex life, which he hid from his wife and only performed with men that he picked up. The witness had told police that the man told him that sometimes the men he picked up wouldn't survive the asphyxiation. Police determined that the man that owned the estate was Herb Baumeister. Initially, his wife refused to believe that her husband was not only secretly gay and constantly being unfaithful to her but also that he was a prolific serial killer. That would change when their 13-year-old son found human bones in the woods that surrounded their home. Police searched the property and found the bodies of seven men. Baumeister, in the meantime, committed suicide, but police believed that he may have been responsible for up to 60 murders including those dubbed the I-70 murders.

The I-70 murders stopped at the same time that Baumeister had bought his large estate, and it is believed that he likely changed his dumping ground to the estate at that time. Although there is significant evidence to indicate that Baumeister was indeed the I-70 killer, those cases remained open and unsolved to this day.

I-70 was again the site of serial murder in 1992, when an unidentified male killed five people in the space of 29 days and then disappeared. All the victims worked in convenience stores or gas stations along the highway, and they were all shot to death. Police believed that this killer was likely arrested for another offence, as in 1993, the murders picked up again, and he shot three more women in the same fashion. Once again, he disappeared and has never been identified.

Q: Were the La Crosse drownings the work of a serial killer or simply tragic accidents?

In the late 1990s and early 2000s, young men were being found in the Mississippi River near the university town of La Crosse. All the young men were confirmed to have drowned, and all had relatively high levels of alcohol in their bodies. For some time, it was believed that these were tragic accidents. Soon, though, strange similarities between the deaths started off the rumor that these murders were in fact the work of a serial killer.

Local police refused to believe this, though, and inferred that it was easier for the public to blame a serial killer than to face up to the fact that the town was guilty of promoting a heavy drinking culture. A lot of things did not add up in the cases, though. The first victim was a very strong swimmer, and his alcohol level was not even that high. It did not make sense that the man would have been unable to get himself out of the river if he had fallen in. Other inconsistencies added to the suspicions, including the fact that one victim who was alleged to have fallen in and accidentally drowned having had his ball cap hung neatly on a nearby post as though someone had placed it there. Another victim had some of his belongings neatly laid out on the floor of a riverboat gift shop. His drowned body was found days later. In the search for another of the victims, a bloodhound had picked up several points along the river where the victim had experienced trauma. That young man's body was also later found in the river.

Experts weighed in saying that drowning would be a highly unusual method of killing for a serial killer, but it is not completely unknown for this to happen, and there are serial killers, like the Tylenol killer, who enjoy watching their victims' deaths from a distance. The similar deaths continued until 2002.

It was revealed, at one point, that a likely suspect had actually come forward but had been dismissed by police. In 1999, a man had walked into a local police department and told them that he was going to be the next Jeffrey Dahmer. Even though police told him to leave, he continued to come back, and they eventually had to take out a restraining order to stop him from coming to the police department. One investigator, though, heard the man claiming that he enjoyed watching young men drown. The man also lived within a few blocks of where many of the young victims had last been seen. He worked in a funeral parlor and had been a member of a fetish website called manunderwater.com for many years. The website caters to gay men who have a fetish about having sex underwater. A private investigator even posed as a young gay man and engaged with the suspect. They shared emails about their fantasies, and a consistent theme came up in which the suspect clearly enjoyed watching the life drain out of a drowning victim's eyes. When this evidence was presented to police, they eventually sat up and took notice and issued a warrant of arrest. On attempting to arrest the man, he took police on a car chase but was eventually arrested and jailed for resisting arrest.

It became clear that the man could not have been the perpetrator of at least one of the crimes because he was in jail at the time. There is no further information available about the progress of this case, but no further arrests have been made in the cases of the drownings at La Crosse. The private investigator's work, though, showed that there definitely are people out there with the potential to become serial killers and who use drowning as their preferred method of killing.

Q: What were the New Haven homicides?

The first murder in a series of child murders that would terrify New Haven, Connecticut, occurred on the 18th of May, 1969. Eleven-year-old Diane Toney was last seen at a parade in town. Her body was found five months later. She had been beaten to death with a rock. In the interim, another young girl had gone missing. Mary Mount was just 10 years old, and her beaten body was found in June of that year.

Shortly after Mary had gone missing, 14-year-old Dawn Cave disappeared after she left her home briefly following a disagreement with her sister. She too had been beaten to death.

The death of a nine-year-old girl in New York would be linked to the first three crimes when the same vehicle was seen in the vicinity of the girls shortly before they went missing. The following year the killer returned to Connecticut, killing 5-year-old Jennifer Noon.

After Jennifer's death, the killer went dormant in that area. In 1972, a truck driver called Harold Meade was arrested and convicted of killing three mentally challenged people by beating them to death with a rock. The similarities to the murders of the young girls, as well as the fact that Meade had allegedly told fellow inmates that the three crimes he was convicted of were only some of his victims, made the man a prime suspect for the child killings.

Witnesses to the abductions of some the girls also picked Meade out of a lineup as the man they had seen. Meade, though, claimed innocence, and there was not much other evidence to link him to the murders.

Sadly, the remains of the very first victim of this series, Diana Toney, would remain unburied for 27 years in the evidence room at the police station. Her family refused to believe that the body had belonged to Diana and would not take possession of the remains. Eventually in 1996, police raised money to provide Diana with a proper burial.

This would not be the last time that New Haven was visited by a child killer, and the second one may well have been the same as the first. Three years after the last murder in the first series, the bodies of girls and young women started to be found again. These murders would continue until 1990 when a man called Roosevelt Bowden was arrested and convicted of some of the second series of murders. The first victims have never received justice.

Q: Which Belgian serial killer played word games with bags of body parts?

In 1998, Belgian authorities found a container filled with skeletal remains. They estimated that there had to have been at least seven bodies as well as five human heads in the containers. This discovery would mark the resurfacing of a serial killer who had haunted the Mons area of Belgium the previous year.

An unidentified killer had played a gruesome game with police in 1997. Thirty different bags of dismembered body parts were found in locations across the area. The locations included a river called Fleuve Trouille, which translates to the River of Jitters, another called the Fleuve Haine or the River of Hate, and another on a road called Chemin de l'Inquietude, which translates to the Path of Worry.

All of the limbs were severed in a very particular way, and this led police to believe that it was indeed the work of the same person. Police could not dismiss the possibility that the murders could have some skewed religious connection as the city of Mons itself has significant ancient religious connections. Mons is a site where in ancient times many beheadings were carried out, and there are monuments throughout the streets to saints related to execution and decapitations. The killer became known as the Butcher of Mons, thanks to their perfectly clean dismemberment of the remains that were found.

Closer inspection showed that the remains had not actually been cut by hand, and instead, an automatic sawing machine like the type used to cut logs had been used. Police initially hoped that this piece of evidence would lead them to the killer as not many people owned a machine like that, and the noise and smell of sawing bone would likely attract attention. This was sadly not the case, though, and the killer remained unidentified.

Some of the victims were identified, although the human jigsaw puzzle that the killer had left behind made it extremely difficult even to figure out how many victims they were dealing with. The victims who were identified mainly seemed to be transients and homeless people.

The Butcher of Mons slowly faded into history, and they have never been identified.

Q: What is Operation Enigma?

Operation Enigma is a British task force set up to address many unsolved murder cases in which sex workers and other vulnerable women were murdered. The operation included what it believed to be several series of murders. One particular series started in 1987 with a 27-year-old sex worker being beaten and strangled in West London. The next victim they believed to be connected to that murder was found in 1991; she had also been beaten and strangled to death. Seven further victims were found over the next seven years. Each had been dumped in a different police district. This indicated that the killer was acting to intentionally confuse the investigation and avoid connections being made between the victims. An FBI profiler working on Operation Enigma classified this killer as being organized, and they would likely not stand out and would easily be able to put their victims at ease. Operation Enigma has had little to no success at this point but continues to attempt to solve these serial murders.

Q: Who is the Bible Belt Strangler?

In 1983, the body of an unidentified red-headed woman was found on the side of the road in West Virginia. This discovery would be the beginning of a series of murders which would eventually end in 1992 but remain unsolved to this day.

The killer in question would alternatively also be called the Redhead Killer because all of his victims had red or reddish-colored hair. The reference to the Bible Belt comes from a name given to certain states in America that are known to be particularly religious. The killer would leave victims in Kentucky, Arkansas, Pennsylvania, Tennessee, and Mississippi. They are believed to have killed at least 11 women during their reign of terror. Sadly, only 4 of the 11 victims would be identified, which is likely one of the main reasons why the killer has also never been identified.

Victimology, as we have indicated previously, is often key to identifying a killer. Often, even if the killer didn't know the victim, just knowing the victim's name helps to identify witnesses that may have seen last movements or a vehicle the victim got into. Many serial killers have been identified simply by similar statements from witnesses or friends and family of the victims.

Q: Will we ever know the true identity of the Zodiac Killer?

The Zodiac killer is probably one of the most infamous unsolved serial murder cases in history. It's right up there with Jack the Ripper in legend quality, as well as the number of books and movies that have been made about the horrendous tales. The man that is still only known as The Zodiac operated in Northern California in the 1960s and 1970s. He is confirmed to have killed five people and injured two. It seems strange that this particular case has captured the imaginations of so many for so long considering he is certainly not the most prolific of killers, nor were his methods the most vicious. What seems to set this case apart from many others, though, is the way that The Zodiac toyed with the police during the time that he was killing. He would send letters and cryptograms to the press and police claiming that if they could only solve the puzzle, they would learn his name. A professor and his wife were able to solve one of the cryptograms that was published in the newspaper, but the only information it offered was that the Zodiac believed he was collecting slaves for the afterlife.

Despite only having five confirmed kills, The Zodiac proudly claimed he had killed 37 people. He mostly targeted couples and only once killed a man on his own who was actually his taxi driver.

The Zodiac disappeared and seemed to stop killing in the 1970s, but many believe that he, in fact, simply reinvented himself and started killing elsewhere. Some think that BTK Dennis Radar's habit of contacting police and the press in a similar way mirrors The Zodiac, and there are theories that Dennis Radar may be The Zodiac.

Over the years, many people have come forward to either claim that they are The Zodiac or to claim that they believe one of their family members may be the serial killer.

All of these claims have, thus far, been refuted, and we still do not know, for sure, who the famed Zodiac killer actually is.

Q: Was the Alphabet child killer responsible for other murders?

In the early 1970s, three child murders took place in Rochester, New York, which would go on to haunt the country interminably. The reason that the murders were referred to as The Alphabet Murders is because the victim's names were all alliterative and started with the same letter as the place they were dumped in. The girls' names were Carmen Colon (dumped in Churchville), Michelle Maenza (dumped in Macedon), and Wanda Walkowicza (dumped in Webster). All murders occurred between 1970 and 1973 when the killer seemingly dropped off the map.

A similar method of victim selection was seen in serial killer Joseph Naso, who murdered four girls in California. Strangely, one of his victims was also called Carmen Colon, and the remaining three were called Pamela Parsons, Tracy Tofoya, and Roxene Roggasch. When police discovered that Naso had also allegedly made a reference to a murder he had committed in Rochester, they tested his DNA against that discovered from the scenes of the Alphabet murders.

Serial killer Kenneth Bianchi was also briefly considered as a suspect for this series as he lived in Rochester, New York, during this period. Bianchi has claimed innocence, and his DNA also does not match the Alphabet killer.

It is likely that DNA will eventually solve this series at some stage as we are starting to see many older cold cases solved through genetic genealogy. It is very possible that the serial killer will no longer be alive when they are identified, but at least, the truth will be known.

Q: How many killers operate on the Highway of Tears?

The Highway of Tears murders are some of the oldest cold serial murder cases in which victims continue to be added to the tally, even today. This stretch of highway runs through British Columbia in Canada and has been the site of more than 40 dumped female victims since 1969. The danger that exists has led authorities to erect billboards along the highway warning women not to hitchhike as there is a killer on the loose. In truth, though, it seems that there may be more than one killer on the loose on the Highway of Tears, and this makes solving these murders all the more difficult.

All of the victims killed on the road are First Nations women, and many believe that this has played a role in the slow progress in the cases and possibly even in the victim selection. Although police acknowledge that they are more than likely looking for multiple individual killers, they do believe that the bulk of the cases can be attributed to one man.

An American serial killer, Jack Fowler, has been accused of being responsible for at least 10 of the murders, and a Canadian serial killer, Cody Legebokoff, has also been convicted of killing many women along this stretch of highway.

Police have admitted that it is unlikely that they will ever solve all of the 40 Highway of Tears murders as too much time has passed, and they have little evidence to hold against suspects. Perhaps the Highway of Tears serial killers made a very smart move in selecting victims that they knew would not be investigated immediately by police. We can only hope that these victims will not have died in vain, and that in future, the murder of women of all ethnic backgrounds will be treated equally by Canadian police.

CHAPTER 9
KILLER COUPLES

Serial killers almost always work on their own. Killing, it seems, is a solitary practice. This is most likely true for most serial killers because their murders are often fantasy based, and, perhaps thankfully, it is uncommon for two killers to share exactly the same fantasy. When lightning strikes twice in the same place, though, and two people find their way to each other and share a murderous dream, the crimes that result are twice as terrifying. As we alluded to when we discussed female serial killers, when a male and female pair up to become a killer couple, it is very often the case that the female is presumed to be the submissive party. In these cases, the female offenders will often claim that they were forced to participate in the crimes, or they were in fear of their own lives. This is hardly ever true, though. As you will see in the cases we present in this chapter, gender plays little role in the hierarchy of evil. Often female serial killers, when paired up with their male counterparts, will be major contributors to the torture portion of the murder.

Especially when the victims are female. The male will most frequently be the one who puts the nail in the coffin, so to speak, and ends the victim's life, but the female partner will often be heavily involved in selecting, luring, and torturing the victims.

In many of these cases, we will be left wondering whether, if those two people hadn't met, either of them would have gone on to commit such acts on their own. In some cases the answer to that question is no, but only because the other person is such a perfect fit for their partner (in all the worst ways of course) that each plays the role of the flame to the other's ticking time bomb.

The dynamics that play out in male/female serial killer relationships are no different in the few cases we have seen of same-sex serial killers who are also in sexual relationships with one another. One partner will always be slightly more dominant in one area, planning perhaps, torture, or victim selection, but the other partner always holds their own in another aspect of the crimes.

One of the most interesting, and often telling parts of a serial killer couple's journey is how they behave after they are arrested. For some, the bond remains eternal, but for many, all bets are off, and it's each to their own. Some of the most horrific serial crimes have been committed by couples, and in this chapter, we will explore what happens when love turns deadly.

Q: Which killer couple was referred to as The Love Slave Killers?

Gerald and Charlene Gallego were a pair of serial killers who terrorized teenagers in Sacramento, California, between 1978 and 1980.

Image 17: Couple

They were convicted of killing 10 teenage girls, but perhaps the worst part of their crimes was that they did not simply kidnap and kill their victims; they kept the girls for varying periods of time during which they subjected them to sexual and physical torture.

Both Gerald and Charlene were married several times each before marrying one another. Gerald was married seven times, and Charlene had two previous husbands before she became Mrs. Gallego. Both parties had prior criminal records with Gerald having been convicted of robbery and Charlene having drug convictions.

They predominantly lured their teenage victims from malls in Sacramento. Once Charlene was able to get them near their van, Gerald would brandish his gun and force the victims into the back. The couple were captured after a witness to one of the kidnappings had written down the license plate number of the Gallegos' van.

As soon as they realized that police had a significant amount of evidence against them, Charlene buckled and offered to testify against Gerald in exchange for a reduction in her prison sentence. Gerald was sentenced to death but died of cancer in 2002 before his death sentence could be carried out.

Charlene Gallego received only 16 years in jail thanks to her plea deal, and she consistently claimed that she was also a victim of Gerald. She alleged that she had attempted to save the lives of many of the victims. She was released from prison in 1997 after having completed degrees in psychology, business, and Icelandic literature.

Q: Which female half of a killer couple committed an armed robbery while eight months pregnant?

Judith Neelley allegedly only began her life of crime when she met her husband Alvin at the tender age of 15. She was eight months pregnant with their twins when she committed a string of armed robberies across the country and was arrested. She gave birth to her twins while in prison on the armed robbery charge.

After Judith's release from prison, the couple began a more serious string of crimes. In September 1982, they abducted a 13-year-old girl from a mall. The girl would be raped and tortured by both Judith and Alvin, but it would be Judith who took charge when it was time to end the poor girl's life. The woman initially experimented with injecting her victim with Drano to see how much it would take to kill her. When this only caused the girl immense pain and did not kill her, Judith eventually fired a single bullet into the back of her head and tossed her body off a cliff.

The couple's second crime involved kidnapping a young couple, but their intention to only keep the female victim was clear from the beginning. The male victim was shot almost immediately, and the couple dumped the man on the side of the road. The female victim was taken back to their house and horrifically tortured and raped before being murdered. What the Neelleys did not know was that the male victim had actually survived and was able to give a full description of the offenders as well as the vehicle.

Police were able to track down the couple and put them under surveillance for three weeks to ensure they did not take any further victims before arresting them. It was revealed that Judith was once again pregnant and again gave birth behind bars. By this time she was just 18 years old herself, but for her horrendous crimes, she was sentenced to death, becoming the youngest woman sentenced to death in the United States. Her sentence would be commuted to life in prison just days after her scheduled execution. Her husband received a sentence of life imprisonment.

Judith was clearly the dominant partner in this relationship and likely the driver behind the crimes. She also had no problem actually committing the murders. She was ranked by a forensic psychiatrist as a category 22 killer, which describes a group of serial torture murderers who are deemed as highly dangerous.

CHAPTER 10
WHEN CHILDREN KILL

The most unthinkable crime must be when a mother kills their own child. It just seems to go against every law of nature for that sacred bond to be broken in such a horrendous way. Crimes that are definitely way up there in shock value, though, are the ones that are committed by minors. It is not uncommon for serial killers to start killing before the age of 18. We know that sometimes they will start with animals, but many skip straight over to human beings, and before they've graduated from high school, are already well on their way to serial killer "status."

The purity of a bond between mother and child is a similar purity to what we, as society, see in children. It seems impossible that an angelic face can hide a murderous mind, but time and again, we are proven wrong. Most often children who kill will start with younger children in their neighborhood or even their own siblings. They are easy to control and accessible. It is also important to remember that most pedophiles are known to commit their first sexual offence before they are 18.

These are not always desires that only come out in adulthood. Very often, the first victims are close to home. Due to the fact that minors are given special treatment in the justice system, they will hardly ever serve hard time, and more often than not, they are back on the streets within a few years only to continue with their murderous deeds.

The very nature of childhood and adolescence makes it extremely difficult to diagnose serious mental illness or personality disorders. The mind is growing and changing at a rapid pace, and the psychiatric community is averse to placing a permanent diagnosis on what might be a temporary problem. In the cases we discuss in this chapter, you will note that, very often, a child that goes on to kill has received some form of psychiatric intervention at as young an age as six. Others receive no attention at all and are simply left to muddle their way through their building fantasies until the bomb explodes. It is very common for adult serial killers to report having killed one or both of their parents or other caregivers. In some cases, this is as a result of serious abuse, but in most it is simply the warped action of a deranged mind.

Q: Which Australian couple committed the Moorhouse murders?

David and Catherine Birnie lived at 3 Moorhouse Street in a suburb of Perth, Australia. They had been living together for a year after Catherine abandoned her six children and husband and moved in with David. They did not marry, but Catherine adopted David's surname. It seems that it was their murderous intentions that had brought them together as, between 1985 and 1986, they perfected their plans before taking their first victim, 22-year old Mary Neilson.

This victim was abducted, chained to a bed in the Moorhouse Street residence, repeatedly raped by David while Catherine watched, and then strangled to death with a nylon cord. The couple buried Mary in a shallow grave in the State Forest.

Image 18: Forest

Their next victim, Susannah Candy, was just 15 years old, and she too was chained to the bed and raped. This time Catherine joined in with the sexual assault, and David asked her to kill the girl to prove her devotion to him. She drugged Susannah and then strangled her to death while she was unconscious. Susannah was buried near their first victim.

The third victim that this couple abducted proved to be a shift in the dynamic of their relationship. Thirty-one-year-old Noelene Patterson was abducted by the couple and held in their house in the same way they had with the other victims. This time, though, David would say that he wanted to keep the woman alive for longer, and three days after she had been taken, she was still alive and being subjected to abuse. David admitted to Catherine that he had grown attached to Noelene and did not want to kill her. Catherine allegedly flew into a jealous rage and told David that if he didn't kill Noelene, she would kill herself. David complied, and interestingly, when they buried Noelene, her grave was far away from the other victims, and Catherine said that she had received great pleasure from shoveling soil onto the dead woman's face.

The Birnie's next victim was 21-year-old Denise Brown, who was held and raped like the other victims and then taken to a pine plantation in the area where she was raped by David again. He then stabbed Denise in the neck. They believed that the girl was dead and proceeded to bury her, but she allegedly sat bolt upright in her grave, and the shocked couple beat her to death with an axe.

Q: Which child killer was the inspiration behind the movie *Natural Born Killers*.

Fourteen-year-old Caril Ann Fugate carried out murders along with her boyfriend, 19-year-old Charles Starkweather. Fugate would allege that Starkweather started the crime spree by killing her stepfather, mother, and younger sister. She says that she returned home to find Starkweather in the house with a gun, and he claimed that her family was being held hostage, and if she complied they would be safe. This claim was strongly refuted when the pair eventually went to trial, and it is believed that Caril may well have had prior knowledge of Starkweather's intention to kill her family. The pair lived in the family home for a few days and refused all visitors. When other family members started to get suspicious, the couple fled. They traveled across Wyoming and Nebraska killing another six people before they were arrested. Fugate admitted only to holding one couple at gunpoint.

Image 19: Scary teenagers

Starkweather had already been sentenced to death and had very little to lose when he admitted that although he had killed most of the victims, Caril Ann Fugate, had in fact, also committed some of the murders herself. Fugate denies this to this day. She served 17 years in prison and went on to marry and live in Ohio. In 2013, Fugate was involved in a serious car accident which took the life of her husband. She attempted to have a pardon passed for her crimes in 2020 so that people would no longer see her as a murderer, but this request was denied by the Nebraska parole board.

Fugate and Starkweather's crimes have become the stuff of pop fiction legend and inspired the movies *Natural Born Killers, The Sadist, Badlands, Kalifornia,* and *Starkweather*. It seems that the young age of both perpetrators as well as the romance they shared makes this story a fascinating tale.

Q: Who is considered to be the world's youngest serial killer?

Amarjeet Sada, an Indian boy, is believed to be the world's youngest serial killer. Sada allegedly started killing when he was seven years old. All of Sada's victims were young babies between the ages of four and eight months. He is believed to have killed his own sister as well as his cousin.

The boy would abduct his victims when their mothers' backs were turned and take them to an open field where he would stone them with bricks until they were dead. He usually buried the babies under piles of leaves so that they would not be found. He was arrested after abducting a baby who was later found dead. One of his neighbors had seen him take the child on this occasion, and police were called.

When questioned, Sada seemed to show absolutely no emotion or remorse for his crimes and admitted to having killed several babies. The exact number of victims is unknown. Psychologists believed that Sada suffered from a personality disorder called Conduct Disorder, which essentially means that they believe he did not know the difference between right and wrong at the time of his crimes. Sada was held in a psychiatric facility for three years and then released.

Q: Which Argentinian serial killer was known as The Big-Eared Midget?

Born in 1896, Cayetano Godino grew up with two alcoholic parents. His father suffered from syphilis, and his mother drank while she was pregnant with him which led to him having serious health issues as a child. He was one of eight children in the household but the only one who went on to become a serial killer.

Godino was seven years old when he attempted to kill a child for the first time. He beat a two-year-old boy severely and dumped him in a ditch. Just a year later, he beat another child with a stone. Police had no idea what to do with him because he was too young for prison, so they sent him home to his parents. At the age of 10, Godino began to masturbate compulsively. His mother had no idea what to do with the child so she informed police. At the time, masturbation was illegal in Argentina, so the boy was sentenced to two months in prison.

When Godino was 16, he began a series of arsons and murders which would eventually claim the lives of four young children. He also kidnapped and assaulted and attempted to kidnap several more children. Godino was eventually arrested and placed in a reformatory where he tried to kill some of the fellow inmates. He was eventually moved to a prison where he continued to attempt to kill fellow inmates and eventually died in 1944 at the age of 48. It is unknown whether one of the other inmates murdered him or if he died of natural causes.

Q: Who is Mary Bell?

One of the most infamous child murderers is a Scottish girl called Mary Bell, who committed two murders at the age of 10. Although by today's standards she would not be considered a serial killer, there is no doubt that the cold-blooded nature of her crimes means that, if she were not caught, she would have continued to kill.

Mary Bell alleged that she had been sexually abused as a child and that she had taken a bad fall prior to the murders, which had resulted in a head injury. Whether or not her decision-making capabilities were affected remains to be seen, but what is known is that she strangled a four-year-old boy to death. She committed this crime on her own, but her second murder was committed with a friend, 13-year-old Norma Bell (no relation). The girls kidnapped a three-year-old boy and strangled him to death. Mary Bell later returned to the body to carve an "M" into the child's skin, cut his hair off, and mutilate his genitals.

Although today we do not class children as psychopaths, when Mary Bell was arrested in 1968, psychiatrists said that she displayed classic symptoms of psychopathy, and she was given an indefinite sentence due to the seriousness of her crime.

In 1980, Mary Bell was released from prison and was given a new identity. This is a practice that is commonly used with serious child offenders so that they can be given the best opportunity to start afresh upon their release. Mary Bell has changed her identity a few times over the years, as journalists have often been able to figure out where she is.

Q: Which serial killer murdered four of her own siblings?

Spanish serial killer Piedad Martinez del Aguila was just 12 years old when her mother appointed her in charge of caring for her 12 siblings. The woman had been having babies one after the other for more than a decade and at that point could no longer care for all of them on her own. She roped in her oldest daughter and put her in charge of feeding and caring for the children.

It is alleged that Piedad soon became unhappy with this arrangement as she was missing out on school and playing with her friends. The young girl did not run away from home or complain, though; instead, she decided to permanently get rid of her siblings. Starting with the neediest children—the youngest—she began to lace the babies' milk with chlorine pellets they kept in the house for cleaning. She had managed to kill four of her siblings before police started to investigate. Of course, they initially suspected Piedad's mother of the murders, but when they observed the dynamic in the household and realized that it was actually the 12-year-old who saw to all the feeding requirements, their focus shifted.

Piedad would attempt to cast blame on her mother for the first three deaths, saying that she had only acted on her orders but agreeing that the fourth murder had been of her own volition. The evidence seemed to prove that her mother was not involved, though. Instead of prison, Piedad was sent to serve out a life sentence in a monastery for wayward women. She is said to have taken up knitting and behaved like a normal child from the moment she was taken away from her family.

Q: Which serial killer is known as The Boston Boy Fiend?

In the 1870s in Boston, Massachusetts, a prolific serial killer was hunting children, but when he was identified, he was certainly not what anyone had expected. Jesse Pomeroy is believed to have tortured and killed at least nine children. His crimes started when he was 11 years old and would continue, despite a brief stint in a reformatory, until he was 14.

After his arrest, Pomeroy confessed to having killed 27 other children. Police were unable to confirm these claims, but, if true, this would make him the most prolific child serial killer of all time.

Q: Who is The Teacup Poisoner?

Graham Young became fascinated with chemistry, and in particular poisons, when he was very young. His father purchased a chemistry set for the boy, not knowing that this would set off murderous intentions. At first he experimented on his classmates, using poison that made them violently ill. When he was 14 years old, though, he attempted to kill his sister by poisoning her tea. The girl was rushed to the hospital, and she survived, but doctors told her father that the girl appeared to have been exposed to a poisonous substance. Graham's father would later admit that he was already suspicious of his son at the point, but he had little evidence, so he simply warned the boy to stop playing with chemicals. He also advised his daughter not to take anything her brother had prepared for her. Although he couldn't know it at the time, Graham's father would later be very sorry that he hadn't taken more direct action.

Image 20: Teacup

Graham did not stop experimenting with poisons or chemicals, and the very next year, at the age of 15, he killed his stepmother. The boy was confined to a psychiatric facility for people that have committed psychiatric offences. He was released nine years later as staff at the facility believed that he had recovered.

Graham, however, had not recovered, and his dark interest in poisons had not died with his first victim either In the 1970s, Graham Young was once again arrested. This time he had almost killed seven people and succeeded in killing one. He was never released again.

Q: Which 13-year-old serial killer stabbed his first victim 58 times?

Also known as *The Warwick Slasher*, Craig Chandler Price committed his first murder at the age of 13. He broke into a neighbor's house and stabbed the female homeowner 58 times with a kitchen knife. This murder remained unsolved, and he went on to break into another neighbor's house two years later, where he stabbed to death a mother and two small children.

Price was not immediately tied to this murder either, but when detectives did a routine interview of the residents of all the surrounding houses, one eagle-eyed detective noticed a large cut on Price's hand. Profilers had by now linked the previous murder to this one and realized they had a serial killer on their hands. Craig Chandler Price was arrested.

He showed no remorse for his acts and even described what his victims' faces had looked like when he stabbed them and also mimicked the cries that the children had made as they died.

He was given a fairly lenient sentence as he was a minor but could not stop himself from behaving badly in prison and was given an additional 10- to 25-years' jail time for these extra offences. Price has allegedly bragged to fellow inmates that as soon as he gets out of jail he will "make history." Price will be eligible for parole in 2020.

Q: Which serial killer led a gang of 500 invisible boys?

Peter Woodrock is known to have displayed signs of psychopathy from a very early age. He was also in foster care by the time he was in his early teens. He would spend most of his time riding his bicycle around the suburbs of Toronto. His foster parents were well aware that he was doing this, but they believed he was simply playing harmless games with the friends he often described to them. The truth was, though, that Peter did not have many real friends; what he did have, though, was 500 imaginary friends. In a fantasy he developed, he was the leader of a gang of 500 invisible boys that he called The *Winchester Heights Gang*.

This seems harmless enough except, as the leader of this "gang," Peter saw fit to start sexually assaulting young children. The number of sexual assault victims he racked up was huge, but Peter stepped up his crimes a level when he started to kill his victims. Between 1956 and 1957, Peter Woodrock murdered three children under the age of ten. He strangled the children but would also insert objects into their genitals and beat them before eventually taking their lives. He was eventually arrested when he was witnessed cycling away from the body of his third victim.

Woodrock was found not guilty by reason of insanity and was sent to a maximum security mental health facility. Over time, Woodrock appeared to be more stable, and he was eventually released to a lower level facility.

Woodrock had by now changed his name to David Michael Krueger, and he fell in love with a fellow patient called Dennis Kerr. The patient rejected his advances, and while he was out on a weekend pass, Woodrock/Krueger convinced a former lover, Bruce Hamill, to help him kill the man who had spurned his advances. The pair stabbed Kerr to death and then Woodrock/Krueger walked into a police station and reported what he had done. He was sent back to the high security facility and passed away there 20 years later.

Q: Was Ed Kemper a child serial killer?

Ed Kemper would go on to become one of the most infamous serial killers in history with his crimes as the Co-Ed Killer, but few know that this deranged serial killer started his murderous spree long before the Co-Ed Killer days.

When Ed was 15, after his parents had divorced and his allegedly abusive mother no longer wanted him to live with her, he was sent to live with his paternal grandparents in California. Shortly after he had arrived, he and his grandmother had been sitting at the kitchen table when they started to argue. Kemper stood up, left the house, and retrieved his grandfather's rifle from the barn. He shot his grandmother twice in the head while she sat at the table. Some sources say that he also stabbed her several times with a kitchen knife. Kemper then sat and waited for his grandfather to return from a shopping trip. When he did, he met the man on the driveway and shot him twice as well, killing him instantly.

He then phoned his mother and asked what he should do. She suggested he call the police, which he did. He was arrested without incident.

Kemper said that the motive for killing his grandmother was just to find out what it would be like. He then said he felt killing his grandfather would be the kindest thing to do so that he didn't have to find out his wife was dead.

Whether an actual diagnosis or just a way for the courts to explain the vilest actions of a 15-year-old, Kemper was diagnosed as a paranoid schizophrenic and sent to a mental health facility. Psychiatrists at the facility who worked with him over the years would eventually cast this diagnosis aside. Kemper was found to be highly intelligent, and he also seemed really good at manipulating the mental health workers around him, who would eventually determine that he was no longer a risk and release him. After his second arrest, for killing 10 young women, Kemper admitted that his high intelligence allowed him to figure out how the psychiatric tests worked and essentially fool them. He also admitted to having spent time in the facility getting to know some of the sex offenders there and quizzing them about how they got caught. By doing this, Kemper was able to learn how to avoid being apprehended.

It is believed that all of Kemper's victims were simply surrogates for the woman he actually wanted to kill—his mother. Shortly before his second arrest, he would achieve this goal too by bludgeoning her to death with a claw hammer, decapitating her, and using her head as a dart board. He was sentenced to eight life sentences, to be served concurrently.

CONCLUSION

The world of serial killers is like a muddy pond—the further in we wade, the darker the waters become. For true crime enthusiasts, serial killers represent the epitome of evil. Their minds are dark and frightening places, and as much as we want to understand them, we come to the realization that we never will. Attempting to truly understand the motivations and actions of serial criminals is simply not possible unless you think like they do. I, for one, hope that I never really do understand them.

It is perhaps this mystery that keeps us coming back. It is that indefinable darkness that sends a chill down our spine when we hear the whisper: "They think it's a serial killer…"

In this book, we started by looking into how law enforcement shape their investigations into serial killers, the specific tools they use, and how these techniques have improved over the years. The more we learn about how serial killers ordinarily behave and how they commit their crimes, the more likely we are to be able to catch them quicker. That is the real goal, isn't it? We will never know how many murderers would have gone on to become serial killers had they not been caught and sentenced to significant prison sentences. We do know for sure, though, that once a person embarks on a psychologically motivated series of murders, they will not stop until law enforcement stops them. If we look at some of the more heinous single murder cases we have seen around the world, it is not difficult to imagine that person going on to commit a similar crime again, if given the opportunity.

Perhaps the more pertinent question is how we stop that very first murder from occurring in the first place, if that is even possible. This is another matter we have delved into in this book: the origins of serial murder, and as we have discovered, it is almost impossible to look at a person in their formative years and say that they will most certainly become a heinous murderer as an adult. Life has too many twists and turns, and there are many opportunities for the right help to be applied at the right time to change someone's path. I have often wondered how the parents of some of the most heinous serial killers in history felt about their child after their crimes were uncovered. Many have stuck by them, of course, but I do not doubt that at least some must have asked themselves what they did to create the monster before them. In some cases, a parent's role in a serial killer's evolution is clear. Systematic and continued abuse from parents and caregivers can forever warp an already damaged mind. The siblings who do not become serial killers cannot be forgotten, though, as they grew up in the same circumstances and did not turn to the vicious behavior that their brother or sister did. They, in turn, must wonder whether those same dark desires lay within them. Just waiting to show themselves.

Once you start to dig down into the world of serial killers you realize how little you actually know. You know the "big" names and much of their stories, but there are so many of these criminals out there that even this book has just scratched the surface.

The gender roles in crime, in general, have always been allocated a certain societal slant. Women are often portrayed as femme fatales, black widows, or victims of coercion, but the women we have discussed in this book blow those theories straight out of the water. Although for many their crimes are not as vicious, bloody, or sexually motivated as a male serial killer, it is clear to see that women are capable of being just as cold hearted as men. Personally, I think the fact that female serial killers so often select victims who are already in a position of dependence, like children and the elderly, makes their crimes almost more despicable. While it is no better to kill a stranger, of course, it takes a special kind of evil to kill someone who looks to you for care.

There doesn't seem to be a country in the world that has not been ravaged at one point or another by the scourge of serial killers. This particular brand of violence and bloodlust knows no societal, racial, or ethnic borders. Some countries have become better than others at solving serial crimes simply because they have had to, and others will always be at a disadvantage due to the amount of resources available to their law enforcement agencies or sometimes the enormous span of their regions. It is interesting to me to see how different countries deal with their serial killers once they are caught. For many, execution is the answer. Take the evil out of society—permanently. Other countries seek to learn from these criminals in order to try and prevent future crimes. Looking at all the different cases we have covered under the "international serial killer" banner, one thing seems to be clear. When a country has a high rate of unemployment, alcohol and drug abuse, and poverty the serial killer victim count always seems to be higher. This could be for a few reasons, but in my mind, at least, it comes down to the vulnerability of victims. When you are hungry, unemployed, addicted, or otherwise hopeless, you are far more likely to fall victim to someone with nefarious intentions. By the same token, it is also far easier for the disappearance and murder of an indigent person to fall through the cracks as they are seen as high risk. So, perhaps in our fight against the rise of serial killers, we should be focusing a little less on predicting who will become a perpetrator and a little more on those who would be easy targets.

It is often interesting to look at lesser-known serial killers and wonder why they are, in fact, not as well-known as their more infamous counterparts. What exactly is it about the serial killers we've never heard of that made their crimes and their victims less newsworthy? I think that much of the time, and it's a sad reality to be sure, that victim profiling plays a role. If a serial killer takes the lives of five college girls, we are probably more likely to hear about him than if he had killed 10 sex workers or

12 homeless people. We might like to deny the fact, but it's true. It's the basis around which the mainstream media build their reporting. It has also been shown that the race of the victims plays a role in how much press attention is received. A serial killer who chooses young white girls from affluent neighborhoods is far more likely to receive press attention than a serial killer that targets young girls from indigenous communities. Although victim selection by serial killers is primarily based on fantasy and availability, it cannot be denied that many of them are well aware of how these inequities can benefit them. It is not uncommon for a serial killer to report that they chose victims that they thought "would not be missed." This is a ridiculous notion, of course, because even if they aren't missed by the media or the public in general, they are most certainly missed by those who love them.

So, this is perhaps another contribution we can make, as a community of people with an interest in true crime. Let us be intimately aware of the cases that draw our focus and ask ourselves if our focus was in fact drawn there or if it was pushed there by societal conditioning. The more we ignore certain types of victims, the more likely serial killers are to continue targeting them.

The only thing more frightening than a story about a serial killer is a story about a serial killer that hasn't been captured. In reality, there are probably more serial killers walking free than there are behind bars! There are serial killers that haven't been caught, and there are murders that have yet to be identified as part of a series. We know how common it is for a killer to be arrested, and only when their DNA is run, or their past movements are tracked, do other crimes start to come to the fore. How many offenders are sitting in jail, right now, guilty of unsolved murders, but refusing to talk, and police have been unable to definitively link them to other suspected cases?

If unsolved serial cases are the most frightening concept, then a close second place must be the idea of a killer couple. Some of the most heinous crimes in history have been committed when two deranged minds meet. How they recognize the evil in one another remains to be seen, but it happens regularly. Perhaps it is simply coincidence and part of a weeding out process; the partners that don't align with the fantasy are either killed or end up divorcing the person. The ones that stick are the ones that think the same and will either gladly look the other way or actively participate in their partner's crimes.

Toward the end of this book, we broached one of the most frightening subjects in true crime: serial murders committed by children. While these crimes are thankfully extremely rare, there are more than enough examples throughout history to fill a book on their own. Of course, these are just the cases we know about, and it is not uncommon for adult serial killers to reveal, after their arrest, that their first murder was committed when they were children. Child killers often get away with their crimes because it is simply so difficult for us to believe that a child would kill, that sometimes even law enforcement is led astray. Society and even judicial systems often don't take deaths caused by children as seriously as they should, sometimes believing that the death must have been accidental. Only later,

The Birnies's final victim and their ultimate downfall was 17-year-old Kate Moir, who they abducted in a similar way to their other victims. The couple had intended to leave Kate handcuffed to the bed for a while as David needed to go to work, and Catherine wanted to buy drugs. David, unfortunately, failed to handcuff the girl properly, and she was able to escape and report the attack to police.

Both Catherine and David were sentenced to four life sentences for their crimes. They stayed in touch after their imprisonment, and it's alleged that they exchanged up to 2,600 letters. In 2005, David Birnie was found dead in his prison cell after having taken his own life. Catherine Birnie has since been denied any possibility of parole, and she is only the third woman in Australian history to have her file marked "never to be released."

Q: Who are the Sunset Strip killers?

Carol Bundy (thankfully no relation to Ted) and her boyfriend Doug Clark were convicted of a series of murders in Los Angeles in 1980. Their victims were predominantly sex workers and teenage runaways.

Carol Bundy had never had a healthy relationship with a man in her life, and by the time she met Doug Clark, she had survived an abusive alcoholic father and three abusive husbands and was in the process of trying to manipulate a married man into leaving his wife for her. Despite the abuse she endured, Bundy was no angel, and she proved herself to be a manipulative and abusive person herself.

Clark moved in with Bundy shortly after they met, and she was not put off by him almost immediately showing a sexual interest in her 11-year-old neighbor. Instead, she helped Clark to lure the girl into their apartment and force her to pose for pornographic photographs. The couple would bring sex workers home to have threeesomes, and Clark soon told Bundy that he wanted to kill a woman during sex.

In 1980, Clark came home and told Bundy that he had killed two teenagers. The woman actually phoned police and advised them of the location of the bodies but stopped short of providing information about Clark's identity.

Just 12 days after the first murders, Clark killed another two women. He decapitated one victim and brought the head home, placing it in the refrigerator. When Bundy saw the head, she after the child has grown up and killed again, is it revealed that the so-called accidental death was very much intentional. It is undoubtedly terrifying to know that a child that is supposed to be the epitome of innocence and sweetness has gone so far wrong in such a short lifetime. Whether a child acts out their violent fantasies while still a child or whether they wait until they are an adult, those fantasies almost always have their roots in those formative years anyway.

The Ultimate Serial Killer Trivia Book is a deep dive into the sometimes murky waters of this popular true crime genre. I think as we have delved into these cases, though, it has become clear that serial murders are about far more than scary stories. There are human beings behind each of the stories we have covered here. The perpetrators, the victims, and their families and friends, are all real people, and I think it is important that we don't forget that. Although the true crime genre, in general, and the topic of serial killers in particular, has always straddled the line between entertainment and morbid curiosity, if we approach these subjects with the right mindset, learning about serial killers can actually be beneficial to society in general.

Serial killers are frightening, offensive, and often downright confounding, but as much as they titillate the mind, I can't seem to stop devouring information about them. This book was the culmination of many years of information gathering, and I hope it has stretched your mind and increased your knowledge base as much as writing it did for me.

As you close the back cover on this book and get ready to settle in for the night, don't forget the stories you've read, and maybe, double-check that you've locked the front door. You never know when evil will come knocking...

reacted completely differently than one would assume and removed the head from the fridge, applied makeup to the face, and helped Clark to perform a necrophilic act with the victim's head. Clark is also known to have killed a young runaway during this time.

Despite her relationship with Clark, Bundy still showed interest in the married man she had been trying to lure before she met her murderous mate. One evening she attended a performance by the man who was a country singer. They had drinks afterward, and her tongue perhaps loosened by alcohol, she confessed some of the murders to the man. He was understandably shocked and indicated that he was going to go to the police. Bundy was not having any of that, and she lured the man into her van on the premise that she wanted to have sex with him, and instead, shot, killed, and decapitated him.

Bundy's loose tongue once again got her into trouble, though, and she confessed to coworkers a few days after the murder. The coworkers called the police, and Bundy laid out all of the horrible truth.

Clark was sentenced to death for his crimes, and Bundy was sentenced to life in prison. She died in prison of heart failure at the age of 61, and Clark was still on death row as of 2015.

Q: Who were the Bloody Benders?

If killer couples are not frightening enough, every now and then the gene pool becomes a cesspool, and an entire family is in on the act. The family that slays together, stays together? In a single year in the 1870s in Kansas, a family called the Benders became the first serial killer family.

John Bender, his wife Elvira, their son, John Jr., and their daughter, Kate, worked together to lure and kill at least 12 people. The Benders ran an inn that was frequented by travelers, and many, it seemed, checked in but never checked out. It is believed that the motive for the murders was a combination of robbery and pure desire to kill. The Benders had built a trapdoor into their dining room floor which fell away into their basement. They would position a guest (who was their intended target) in a chair seated over the trapdoor. During dinner, one of the men would sneak up behind the victim with a large hammer and strike them in the head. At this moment, one of the women would pull on a lever that opened the trapdoor, and the victim would fall into the basement. The killer family would then finish off the victims in the basement and steal everything of value from them before disposing of their bodies.

The Bloody Benders' devious antics came to an end when one of their victims managed to escape and alerted police. The Benders went on the run, and huge rewards were put on their heads. It is believed that John Jr. died of natural causes during their escape, but the truth about the final fate of the remaining Benders is steeped in legend. Many people attempted to lay

REFERENCES

Bonn, S. (2014, October 24). *5 myths about serial killers and why they persist* [Excerpt]. Scientific American. https://www.scientificamerican.com/article/5-myths-about-serial-killers-and-why-they-persist-excerpt/

Farber, T. (2019). *Blood on her hands.* Jonathan Ball Publishers.

Margaritoff, M. (2019, May 8). *The inside story of Ted Bundy's execution, last meal, and final words.* All That's Interesting. https://allthatsinteresting.com/ted-bundy-execution

Mosti, C., & Coccaro, E. F. (2018). Mild traumatic brain injury and aggression, impulsivity, and history of other- and self-directed aggression. *The Journal of Neuropsychiatry and Clinical Neurosciences, 30*(3), 220–227. https://doi.org/10.1176/appi.neuropsych.17070141

Philbin, T., & Philbin, M. (2009). *The killer book of serial killers : incredible stories, facts, and trivia from the world of serial killers.* Sourcebooks.

Pistorius, M. (2005). *Strangers on the street: Serial homicide in South Africa.* Penguin Books.

Pistorius, M. (2005). *Profiling serial killers.* Penguin Books. (Original work published 2005).

Ramsland, K. (2012, March 16). *Triad of evil.* Psychology Today. https://www.psychologytoday.com/za/blog/shadow-boxing/201203/triad-evi

IMAGE REFERENCES

Image 1: Crime scene tape (n.d.). Retrieved from https://pixabay.com/illustrations/crime-scene-man-view-model-1240780/

Image 2: Forensics (n.d.). Retrieved from pixabay.com/photos/zurich-cantonal-police-crime-scene-3227506/

Image 3: Frightening child (n.d.). Retrieved from https://pixabay.com/photos/horror-creepy-weird-halloween-fear-4217529/

Image 4: Arrested (n.d.). Retrieved from https://pixabay.com/photos/police-arrest-detention-handcuffs-2122376/

Image 5: Healthcare worker (n.d.) Retrieved from https://pixabay.com/photos/doctor-dentist-dental-clinic-1149149/

Image 6: Playing cards (n.d.). Retrieved from https://pixabay.com/photos/playing-cards-poker-bridge-game-1201257/

Image 7: Postboxes (n.d.). Retrieved from https://pixabay.com/photos/letter-box-spooky-scary-ghost-2020123/

Image 8: Toolbox (n.d.). Retrieved from https://pixabay.com/photos/toolbox-industrial-instrumentation-1582313/

Image 9: Femme fatale (n.d.). Retrieved from https://pixabay.com/photos/noir-femme-fatale-glamour-retro-3783057/

Image 10: Female wrestlers (n.d.). Retrieved from https://pixabay.com/photos/wrestling-athletes-match-strength-680056/

Image 11: Homeless child (n.d.). Retrieved from https://pixabay.com/photos/boy-lonely-asian-sad-alone-child-4658244/

Image 12: Hammer (n.d.). Retrieved from https://pixabay.com/photos/hammer-nails-wood-board-tool-work-1629587/

Image 13: Baby (n.d.). Retrieved from https://pixabay.com/photos/babe-smile-newborn-small-child-boy-2972221/

Image 14: Knife (n.d.). Retrieved from https://pixabay.com/photos/knife-stabbing-stab-kill-murder-316655/

Image 15: Hospital (n.d.). Retrieved from https://pixabay.com/photos/hospital-labor-delivery-mom-840135/

Image 16: Child being led away (n.d.). Retrieved from https://pixabay.com/photos/father-and-son-walking-love-child-2258681/

Image 17: Couple (n.d.). Retrieved from pixabay.com/photos/couple-romance-love-kiss-lovers-3064048/

Image 18: Forest (n.d.). Retrieved from https://pixabay.com/photos/forest-mist-nature-trees-mystic-931706/

Image 19: Scary teenagers (n.d). Retrieved from https://pixabay.com/photos/bite-a-vampire-couple-spooky-1390678/

Image 20: Teacup (n.d.). Retrieved from https://pixabay.com/photos/cup-tee-porcelain-drink-decor-829527/

claim to having killed the three remaining family members, but no one was ever able to provide proof of their claims. This murderous family may well have walked off into the sunset to start again somewhere else.

Q: Which killer couple counted their own daughter among their victims?

Fred and Rosemary West are possibly one of the most notorious killer couples. Rosemary was Fred's second wife, and the couple would go on to murder Fred's first wife in order to cover up the fact that Rose had murdered Fred's daughter with this woman.

The couple are believed to have killed at least 11 victims together, and it is likely that Fred killed many more on his own. Both Fred's and Rosemary's childhoods were disturbed and abusive. Fred's father was an extreme disciplinarian, and his mother suffered from various untreated mental conditions. Fred's father is alleged to have molested his daughters, but when Fred was accused of raping his sister and then it emerged that he had been molesting other young girls in the area, he was expelled from the family home. He would go on to marry his first wife soon after this.

His first marriage was fraught with abuse, and his wife Rena would soon leave him. Fred met Rosemary when she was just 15 years old. Her parents were not happy with the relationship, and her father, who had been sexually abusing Rosemary for years himself, threatened to phone the police if the much older man didn't stay away from his daughter.

Rosemary would care for Fred's daughters with his first wife, and they soon started having children of their own too. The woman is alleged to have started working as a sex worker. She was extremely sadistic and abusive to the children, and while

Fred was serving a prison sentence for fraud and robbery, she killed Charmaine, his oldest daughter. She cruelly told Fred's other daughter that their mother had come to fetch the child and left her behind. She would only find out as an adult that her sister was in fact dead.

Rosemary was mercilessly abusive to her children, and the type of abuse she inflicted upon them would later make police believe that, when it came to their murder victims, Rosemary had been the one to initiate the torture, while Fred was only interested in raping the women. The West couple rented out rooms in their house, and many of their victims were lodgers or nannies they had hired to care for the children. All their victims were viciously abused, raped, and then murdered in a variety of ways. Some of the victims were encased in concrete in the basement of their home, while others were buried in a nearby field. Horrifyingly, once the basement could no longer hold any more bodies, the Wests moved some of their children down there and made it into a makeshift bedroom for them so that they could fit more lodgers in the upper rooms.

The Wests' oldest biological daughter, Heather, would also fall victim to the couple, as she had allegedly wanted to leave the home, and they feared that she would tell police about what she had experienced in the home. Fred has always claimed that Rosemary killed the girl, and her siblings confirmed that the last time they saw Heather she was sitting on a couch at home, with her mother. They all left the house for school, and when they returned, their mother told them that Heather had gotten a job and left. For many years, they believed that their sister was alive.

Fred was known to have assisted with the disposal of Heather's body. He would occasionally taunt the children when they misbehaved by saying if they didn't watch out they would "end up under the porch like Heather."

Sexual abuse against the West children was rife, and it would be the rape of one of the younger girls that would eventually spark an investigation into the goings on at their address—25 Cromwell Street. The child abuse charges would initially go nowhere, but the conversations one detective had with the children made it so that she could not let things rest. When the detective was unable to find Fred's first wife, their daughter Charmaine, or the Wests' daughter Heather, the stories the children told about the disappearance of these relations made the detective sure that they were buried at the premises. An eventual search and excavation of 25 Cromwell Street would reveal something even more heinous, and both Fred and Rosemary were arrested.

Rosemary would go on to claim that Fred had been responsible for everything, and that, in most cases, she hadn't known about the murders. When she did know, she claimed that she was so terrified for her own safety that she had no choice but to assist Fred. This would be proven to be untrue. Rosemary was a willing participant and even the aggressor in many cases.

Fred West would go on to commit suicide in prison leaving Rosemary holding the bag. The woman was sentenced to life imprisonment and continued to try to manipulate her children from prison.

Twenty-five Cromwell Street would eventually be completely demolished, and a memorial to the victims murdered there now stands where the house of horrors once did.

Q: Which killer couple is known as the Moors Murderers and recorded audio of the torture of one of their victims?

Myra Hindley and Ian Brady are another British killer couple whose crimes have become infamous over the years. The couple killed at least five children between 1963 and 1965 and buried them on the expansive tracts of land in Manchester referred to as the Moors.

The couple met at their workplace in 1961, and Hindley immediately became obsessed with Brady. Hindley would always claim, just as Rose West had, that she had been controlled, manipulated, and abused by her partner, and this had led to her involvement in his crimes. The evidence would prove otherwise.

Myra would usually lure the children they kidnapped into their vehicle. Presumably because she was a woman, the children felt at ease. It was only once they asked to be released from the vehicle or were taken back to the house that they would realize that they were in trouble.

The children were all tortured and raped by both Brady and Hindley, had photographs taken of their abused bodies, and were then murdered in a variety of ways. After their arrests, police found a 16-minute audio tape in which one of their young victims cried for her mother and pleaded for her life.

Photographs that the couple had taken at the Moors allowed police to locate many of the graves, but one victim, John

Kilbride, has never been found, and he is believed to still be buried somewhere on the Moors.

Both killers were convicted and sentenced to whole-life tariffs, which under British law means they would never be released from prison. Hindley passed away in prison at the age of 60 from natural causes. Brady passed away at the age of 79, also from natural causes.

Weirdly, in the initial years of Hindley's imprisonment she was briefly held in the same prison as Rosemary West. It is alleged that the two women became very close and may have even been lovers at one point. Yet another killer couple!

Q: Which serial killer couple met at a soup kitchen?

The odd pair of Otis Toole and Henry Lee Lucas met at a soup kitchen in 1976. The pair seemed to immediately recognize the darkness in one another and began a sexual relationship.

Toole would later claim that he had committed 1,006 murders with Lucas. Lucas, for his part, confessed to over 100 murders, but many of these confessions have since been proven untrue.

Although Lucas had already committed several crimes before meeting Toole, he seemed to settle down for a while after meeting the man and even lived with the Toole family and worked as a roofer. Toole would be convicted of killing four people. Whether any of these murders really occurred with Lucas as his partner is unknown, but Lucas claimed he had been present at many of Toole's murders.

Both of these killers seemed to be far more interested in notoriety than anything else, and after their eventual arrest for various crimes, they would both provide several false confessions.

Q: Who were the Ken and Barbie Killers?

Paul Bernardo and Karla Homolka were a Canadian serial killer couple who had such wholesome appearances that they were compared to Ken and Barbie. The reality of their crimes, though, is far less wholesome.

Paul Bernado was a serial rapist before he met Karla. In 1987, Bernado terrified the suburbs of Ontario as the Scarborough Rapist. During the five years that Bernado was active on his own, he raped and attacked at least 19 women. Bernado met Homolka when he was 23 and she was just 17. The pair soon discovered that they shared some of the same demented fantasies, and it is believed that Homolka was well aware of Bernado's crimes as the Scarborough Rapist and encouraged him to continue. The pair became engaged, and their sex life revolved around sadomasochistic fantasies where Bernado was the master, and Homolka was his willing slave.

It is alleged that their crimes together started when Bernardo began to complain that Homolka had not been a virgin when they met, and because of this he wanted to be able to have sex with her 15-year-old sister, Tammy, who was a virgin. Homolka encouraged the idea and told Bernado that she wanted him to have her sister's virginity as a Christmas present. On the 23rd of December, 1990, Homolka spiked her sister's drink at a Christmas party at her parents' home. While the rest of the family slept, the couple held a halothane-soaked cloth over Tammy's mouth and took turns raping her. Homolka filmed the entire event. When Tammy began to vomit and choke on the vomit, the couple panicked and called an ambulance. Despite the chemical burn on the teenager's face, her eventual death was ruled an accidental death from alcohol poisoning as the drugs that her sister had given her were not picked up in her system.

One would think that the death of her own sister would have terrified Homolka into leaving Bernado, but quite the opposite happened, and she and Bernado would soon be living together. The very next year, Homolka brought a teenager home that she had met at work. The couple drugged the girl and raped her while she was unconscious, again videotaping the events. This victim survived and had no memory of what happened to her. She would only be made aware of the horrific events of that night after the couple were arrested, and police found the videotape of her assault.

On the day that Bernado and Homolka got married, another of their murder victims was found in Lake Gibson. The teenager, 14-year-old Leslie Mahaffy, had been kidnapped two weeks before the couple's wedding. They had kept her alive for several days, torturing, abusing, and raping her, and then killed her and dismembered her body. They had set the body parts into concrete blocks, but rather than sinking to the bottom of the lake as they had hoped, some of the smaller pieces had floated.

It would be another year until the couple killed again. This time, they left the body of their victim on the roadside. Part of this victim's torture had been to shave her head while they raped her.

Police were able to connect two of these murders and had a composite drawing made up of the man witnesses had seen with the victims. While this investigation was ongoing, Homolka had left Bernado after he had turned violent with her and beaten her viciously. Bernado's DNA would be found to be a match to samples taken from the Scarborough Rapist victims.

Homolka almost immediately turned against Bernado after she too was arrested and agreed to testify against him in exchange for a plea bargain. This deal was made before police had discovered the videotapes that had been made by Homolka proving that she was not a victim as she had claimed.

Homolka got off particularly easily with a 12-year prison sentence and was released from jail in 2005. She remarried and now has children of her own. What her parents' reaction was to the knowledge that their own daughter had raped and killed her sister is unknown.

Bernado was sentenced to life in prison, but he was not denied the possibility of parole. After 25 years in prison in 2018, he applied for parole, but it was turned down as he has never shown any remorse for his actions.

Q: Which killer couple set their crimes up as a spelling game?

Gwendolyn Graham and Catherine Wood met when they worked as nurses at a Grand Rapids frail care facility for the elderly. They soon became involved in a romantic relationship, and it is alleged that it was Graham who came up with a twisted game for the pair to play.

It was decided that they would suffocate their elderly patients to death in a very particular order. According to the first letter of the victim's first name, the pair planned to kill six patients to spell out the word "murder."

The pair managed to complete the first five letters of the word before Graham was transferred to another facility. Whether the transfer was the facility's way of getting rid of someone they believed to be a threat to their patients or whether it was simply a coincidence is unknown. Either way, when Wood discovered that the hospital Graham had been transferred to was a pediatric facility, she became concerned that the woman would start killing children, and she confessed to her husband and eventually to police.

Both women were arrested, and Wood was sentenced to 20 years behind bars while Graham was given life in prison as her sentence.

Q: Which sadomasochistic couple killed eight people over two years in six states?

Alton Coleman and Debra Brown started their killing spree in 1984 by killing three children. They then killed an elderly couple by beating them to death with a pipe and would kill another three people before they were eventually arrested when one victim survived and reported their ordeal to police.

Although the couple may have thought it clever to kill in so many different states, likely believing it would be more difficult for police to catch them, this actually backfired on them when it came to trial. Authorities in all the different states convened and decided that they would try the couple in Ohio as it had the death penalty.

It was alleged that the pair had a master and slave relationship with Coleman being the dominant force. Coleman was sentenced to death for his part in the crimes and was executed in 2002, and Brown was sentenced to life in prison for her role.

Q: Who is the oldest couple in American history to receive the death penalty?

Faye and Ray Copeland were 69 and 76 years old respectively when they were convicted of murdering five men at their ranch in Missouri. Ray Copeland was a con man who purchased livestock with fake checks. After getting into trouble for fraud for these schemes, he decided to kill off the people he was buying the livestock from instead.

By the time someone spotted human remains on his ranch and advised the police, Ray had killed five men. Faye Copeland claimed that she had nothing to do with the murders and that she was a victim of abuse by her husband. This would be proven as untrue when investigators found a quilt that the woman had made using all the murder victims' clothes.

Both Faye and Ray were sentenced to death for their crimes. Ray died of natural causes in prison in 1993, and Faye's death sentence was commuted to life imprisonment. She was allowed medical parole in 2002 after she suffered a stroke and was transferred to an assisted living facility where she passed away at the age of 82.

Q: Who were the Lonely Hearts Killers?

Nineteen-forties killer couple Raymond Fernandez and Martha Beck became known as the Lonely Hearts Killers after luring victims with lonely hearts ads in newspapers. When Beck met Fernandez, she became so obsessed with him that she ended up abandoning her own children to be with him. The arrogant Fernandez lapped up her devotion, and soon they set about making even their most deviant desires come true.

The ads the couple placed called for young females to respond to a possible relationship with Fernandez. When the women arrived at the couple's home, Beck would pretend to be Fernandez's sister as this usually set the victims at ease knowing that there was another woman in the house Inevitably, any woman that entered the couple's home did not leave alive, and the remains of at least 20 women were eventually found buried in their basement.

Families of the missing victims alerted the police to their connection to Fernandez, and the couple was arrested. Both parties were sentenced to die in the electric chair, and both were known to make loud declarations of their love for one another as their last words.

Q: Which female part of a killer couple aided in gouging her own goddaughters' eyes out as part of her crimes with her husband?

Russian serial killer couple Inessa Tarverdiyeva and Roman Podkopaev were believed to have murdered at least 30 people in six years. Tarverdiyeva's daughters from a previous marriage, who were 25 and 13 at the time, also took part in the crimes.

The couple carried out a wide range of crimes besides their murders, including robberies. They would often target the homes of rich families. In 2009, they broke into a home and killed a husband and wife as well as their two children. All they stole was a laptop, hairdryer, and a camera.

They also targeted Tarverdiyeva's own goddaughters, waiting until they knew their parents were not home, breaking in, and torturing the two teenage girls for hours, before gouging their eyes out and killing them.

Roman would be killed in a shootout with police when the couple was arrested, but Tarverdiyeva and her daughters were given life sentences for their roles in the crimes.

www.ingramcontent.com/pod-product-compliance
Lightning Source LLC
LaVergne TN
LVHW012042070526
838202LV00056B/5564